Missions
in the age of
the Spirit

John V. York

Stanley M. Horton, Th.D.
General Editor

LOGION
P R E S S

Springfield, Missouri
02-0464

4th Printing 2011

Logion Press books are published by Gospel Publishing House.

Library of Congress Cataloging-in-Publication Data
York, John V., 1944–
  Missions in the age of the spirit / John V. York; Stanley M. Horton, general editor.
      p. cm.
Includes bibliographical references and index.
ISBN 0-88243-464-0 (pbk.)
    1. Missions—Theory—Biblical teaching. 2. Missions—Biblical teaching. 3. Assemblies of God—Doctrines.
I. Horton, Stanley M. II. Title.

BV2073.Y67 2000
266—dc21
                                              00-035229

To my wife, Joy, in loving gratitude for her untiring assistance in helping this book to become a reality

Contents

Foreword

What missionary-scholar John York has preached and taught on the African continent for the past 25 years is finally in print. His passion, which has influenced countless thousands, has been set down in a volume of richness that may be mined at leisure.

Dr. York is clear about his conviction—that the Bible must be read missiologically. This conviction has been reinforced by 25 years of missionary experience, lived out in a disciplined and ever-sharpening focus on the biblical truth that motivates him. "God's plan has always been a redemptive blessing of the nations . . . . [and] all of Scripture should be read with a view toward its development of the theme of God's promise to bless the nations" (introduction to unit 1).

Missions in the Age of the Spirit is a wonderful model of Pentecostal scholarship. It has not been written while removed from the subject matter. Whether in academic settings in the West or in the Bible colleges of Africa, John York's passion for the *missio Dei* is obvious. Because of his firm belief in the authority of Scripture, Dr. York, in unit 1 of this volume, surveys the mission theme present throughout Scripture, which, he affirms, is the lens of continuity which brings the Bible into focus. And what is the logical and proper response to the *missio Dei* so authoritatively described in the biblical text? Participation.

Not only has Dr. York "participated" in the *missio Dei*, he has made it his lifelong passion to challenge every Christian to respond in kind. This is truly scholarship done in Pentecostal fashion. Touched by God we look to the Bible for clarification of what has happened to us and how we must respond. We discover a mission that God has had since before the foundation of the world and an empowerment that compels us to join the *missio Dei* in God's redemptive pursuit of the nations. Pentecostal biblical reflection done in the midst of ministry sharpens understanding of the Bible and emboldens further witness to the God who is for all nations.

As we enter the twenty-first century many church leaders and missions agencies across the Christian spectrum wrestle with their task's shape for the future. At times the challenges of the future have stripped missions leaders of any sense of history, but ahistorical approaches to the future are doomed from the beginning. In unit 2 Dr. York affirms that God has been active in His redemptive mission between the era of the apostles and the era of modern missions. And his historical perspective testifies to the value of understanding the past in order to discern the future, particularly that of mission endeavor.

Unit 3 looks to the future as it describes the Pentecostal missionary ethos, including the personal call and life of the missionary. In these chapters you will glimpse the author himself, whose words are written from a life of missionary experience, a heart for the lost, and a bedrock belief in the necessity of Spirit baptism to empower candidates for the *missio Dei*. I pray that the passion of John York the missionary found on these pages will correspond to your heart.

Missions in the Age of the Spirit hazards a challenging journey. The biblical insights, the historical and missiological perspectives, and the passionate Pentecostal spirituality may call the reader to accountability. And the final words of this volume may very well echo and re-echo in the conscience: "Let all who contemplate Christ's mission be filled with the Holy Spirit, be prepared to the fullest extent possible, be confident of divine blessing, and then run to the battle. And *run to win!*"

Byron D. Klaus, D.Min.
President
Assemblies of God Theological Seminary
Springfield, Missouri USA

Preface

I will never forget the excitement of missions convention time in my childhood: the films, the booths, and most of all the stirring missionary sermons followed by soul-searching prayer times.

Though a lot of missions work has taken place since then, Christ has not yet returned. Because Christ commissioned the Church to complete His mission to disciple all nations, the logical conclusion is that the missionary task of the Church is as yet incomplete and that its completion should remain the Church's highest priority. But what is this task? How should it be approached? What contribution can Pentecostal believers make to an understanding of this task and to its accomplishment? These questions inform many discussions of missions, and these are the questions that drive this book.

My wife and I were privileged to work for many years within the training ministries of the Nigerian Assemblies of God. We would likely be happily serving there still had a call not come to direct a training ministry as part of the continental Decade of Harvest thrust. As part of this ministry, I began teaching missions, especially the biblical theology of missions, in graduate programs in both Africa and America. Though other forums began to open for this message, it came as a surprise to me when Loren Triplett, then executive director of the Assemblies of God Division of Foreign Missions, asked me to write this book.

Something should be said about the receptive environment within Africa, where much of this material has been presented to students, teachers, and church leaders. Throughout the last quarter of the twentieth century, the African church as a whole has expanded rapidly. Its almost insatiable urge to evangelize, however, has often been approached with an implicit understanding that missionary senders come primarily from the West while the receivers are those living elsewhere. When those from Africa's expanding churches come to grips with the biblical foundations that undergird Christ's teaching on worldwide mission, the sense of release approaches an emotion of liberation. The Pentecostal nature of the churches within my experience seems to have specially prepared them for the challenge of missions in much the same way it did the Pentecostal churches of the Apostolic Era.

Two thoughts taken from Paul's missionary epistle to the Colossians further explain the orientation of this book. First, Paul was not reluctant to mention his own calling to God's mission (1:1,23,25).[1] This sense of personal involvement, which I identify with, continues to be characteristic of much that is written about mission. Second, Paul identifies "the glorious riches of this mystery" as "Christ in you, the hope of glory" (1:27). This verse is dealing with the gospel going to the Gentiles (including Paul's Colossian readers), and the "you" is plural. The presence of Christ within all nations—Jew and Gentile—will ultimately lead to His receiving the glory He is entitled to (Eph. 1:6,14). It is in an active quest for this glory that any church may find its mission.

---

[1]See Bernard Rossier, "Colossians," in *Galatians–Philemon*, ed. Stanley M. Horton, vol. 8 of *The Complete Biblical Library: The New Testament Study Bible* (Springfield, Mo: The Complete Biblical Library in cooperation with Gospel Publishing House, 1986), 253.

A word may be in order concerning my use of a term frequently used in missions literature: *missio Dei* (Latin for "missions of God"). I am not attempting to follow any of the historic schools of thought of the last century.[2] I simply attempt to demonstrate that God is indeed a God of mission, that the Scriptures give a diachronic unfolding of that mission, and that though the entire Bible is directly or indirectly a statement of God's mission, the primary focus from Genesis to Revelation remains the proclamation of the gospel to all nations. This is what I call *missio Dei*.

Special thanks are in order to the many from within the Division of Foreign Missions and the African Theological Training Service network who have encouraged this book's completion. I would also like to gratefully acknowledge the spiritual and practical contributions the African church has made to my understanding of how churches and individuals should respond to Christ's call.

May these pages provide a helpful beacon to inquiring readers who would take seriously the challenge of missions in the age of the Spirit.

John York
Director, Africa Theological Training
Service

---

[2]David J. Bosch, *Transforming Mission: Paradigm Shifts in Theology of Mission* (Maryknoll, N. Y.: Orbis Books, 1991), 389-393. Bosch traces the development of the "mission of God" concept in missions thinking within the twentieth centry: First, *missio Dei* was seen as the Father sending the Son and the Father and Son sending the Spirit. Then, this "traditional view" was modified to emphasize the Father, Son, and Holy Spirit sending the church into the world. Later, some developed a wider view in which the emphasis was upon all that God was doing in the world with less emphasis upon the church. Still later, some came to the view that mission was only God's work in the world, thus excluding the church from participation in the mission of God.

In line with the usage of both the KJV and the NIV, "Lord" is used in capitals and small capitals where the Hebrew of the Old Testament has the personal, divine name of God, Yahweh (which was probably pronounced 'ya-wa).[3]

In quoted Scripture, words the authors wish to emphasize are in italics.

For easier reading, Hebrew, Aramaic, and Greek words are all transliterated with English letters.

These abbreviations have been used:

KJV: King James Version
NASB: *New American Standard Bible*
NEB: *The New English Bible*
NIV: New International Version
TEV: Today's English Version

STANLEY M. HORTON
GENERAL EDITOR

---

[3]The Hebrew wrote only the consonants YHWH. Later traditions followed the New Latin JHVH and added vowels from the Hebrew for "Lord" to remind them to read *Lord* instead of the divine name. This was never intended to be read "Jehovah."

UNIT 1:
READING THE BIBLE
MISSIOLOGICALLY

Christians believe that God has chosen to reveal himself to humankind through His written Word, the Bible. As Paul wrote in 2 Timothy 3:16, "All Scripture is God-breathed and is useful for teaching, rebuking, correcting and training in righteousness." The Bible in turn bears witness to Jesus Christ, the living Word. Jesus taught, " 'You diligently study the Scriptures because you think that by them you possess eternal life. These are the Scriptures that testify about me' " (John 5:39).

The Scriptures further indicate that God has planned for this testimony about Jesus Christ to be given to the entire inhabited earth (Gen. 12:3; Matt. 24:14; 28:18–20). It is my position that this plan provides the overall theme the Bible is organized around. Some would see "kingdom of God," "salvation," or some other phrase or word as the theme of the Bible. While leaving this debate to others, I believe that the advance of the Kingdom through the preaching of the gospel (rather than "kingdom" in some abstract sense) is best seen as the theme. The Bible tells this story of an advancing

19

Kingdom, the mission of the triune God: providing redemption, finding the lost, and then using them to mediate kingdom blessings to those yet lost. In the study of missions, the Latin term for mission of God, *missio Dei,* refers to God's plan to bless the nations through the gospel of Jesus Christ.

Unit 1 deals with the mission of God diachronically (*dia* = across, *chronos* = time). That is, the mission of God will be traced throughout successive time periods in order to demonstrate that God's plan has always been a redemptive blessing of the nations. In its ultimate fulfillment, this blessing would come through Jesus Christ, the offspring (Heb. *zera`*, "seed") promised first to Eve (Gen. 3:15), then to Abraham (Gen. 22:18), to Isaac (Gen. 26:4), and to Jacob (Gen. 28:14). I concur with Walter C. Kaiser in viewing this mission of God as a single *promise plan* uniting all Scripture.[1]

Since God has always had a mission, the Bible should be read missiologically. That is, all of Scripture should be read with a view toward its development of the theme of God's promise to bless the nations through the promised seed. It is as Christian believers recognize God's mission that they may purpose to participate in fulfilling that mission. The first task therefore is to trace *missio Dei* throughout the Scriptures.

---

[1]Walter C. Kaiser, *Toward an Old Testament Theology* (Grand Rapids: Zondervan Publishing House, 1978), 1–40.

Chapter 1:

Missio Dei in the Pentateuch and Historical Books: God's Plan Revealed

Pentateuch

CREATION

The Genesis record reveals an intentional act of creation by a purposeful God. In broad, swift strokes, a portrait of creation is painted in which God is the uncreated Sovereign whose domain is universal, whose will is supreme, whose power is limitless, and whose design is perfect. The remainder of Scripture will repeatedly refer to creation as having established the right of God to rule as King over all peoples. Those willing to serve the Creator are invited into covenant participation in "the kingdom of light" (Col. 1:12). Those unwilling to serve the Creator are regarded as rebellious followers of "the dominion of darkness" (Col. 1:13). The crowning act of creation is humankind, male and female, who alone of all creation are made in God's image (Gen. 1:26–27).

IMAGE OF GOD

There are two great missiological implications to the statement that humankind is made in God's image:

21

First, it demonstrates humankind's capacity to fellow-ship with God. Though this account precedes the Fall (Gen. 3), it lays the groundwork for the reconciliation that will follow. Since human beings are made in God's image, then fallen humankind may be restored to fellowship with Him. There can be no group of people who by reason of ethnicity or location are beyond God's purview, incapable of responding to the overtures of divine grace.

This understanding of the image of God becomes a foundation for Christ's Great Commission that will follow in the New Testament (Matt. 28:19–20). Since God has made everyone in His image, then His Son means to include everyone when He mandates making disciples "of all nations." Though God is King over all creation, the drama of His kingdom is told primarily in terms of the extension of His rule over the world of human beings. Because all peoples are equally created in His image, all are necessarily to be subjects of His rule. Thus there must be a mission of God to proclaim redemption to all so that all may have the opportunity to participate as loyal subjects.

The second great implication is that people are created with the capability of representing their Creator. Once God created humankind in His image, He commissioned them, male and female, to rule the world of creation (Gen. 1:28). This rule is illustrated in Adam's naming of the animals (Gen. 2:19–20). In this text, and still in most cultures, naming implies authority. When God brought the animals He had created for Adam to name, God was assigning the prerogatives of ownership to Adam as to a viceroy.[1] Thus, Genesis 1:28 stands as an Old Testament antecedent to Paul's New

---

[1]Eugene H. Merrill, "A Theology of the Pentateuch," in *A Biblical Theology of the Old Testament*, ed. Roy B. Zuck (Chicago: Moody Press, 1991), 14–16; Walter C. Kaiser, *Toward an Old Testament Theology* (Grand Rapids: Zondervan Publishing House, 1978), 73–76.

Testament teaching that Christian believers are ambassadors for Christ (2 Cor. 5:20). In stating that all human beings are made in His image, God has stated that all are created equally qualified to be His representatives in accomplishing the objectives of His kingdom. Later, in the Book of Acts, both Jewish and Gentile believers are baptized in the Holy Spirit as evidence that all nations share the same Great Commission to serve as God's agents in discipling the remaining nations.

To summarize, I would say that God's creation of humankind in His image establishes both the scope and agency of God's mission. God's mission will be to all peoples, and it will be accomplished through the redeemed of all peoples. To expect less is to miss these two foundational implications of the creation of human beings in the image of God.

MISSIO DEI AS BLESSING THE NATIONS

Three major events following creation serve as preparation for God's declaration of mission. In each case, a seeming hindrance to the accomplishment of God's mission is answered by a strong word of promise.

First comes the tragic fall of humankind into sin (Gen. 3:1–19), answered by a promised "seed" (KJV) of woman, who would crush the head of the serpent (Gen. 3:15). This promise becomes the foundation of God's plan to bless the nations. Events following the Fall define the mission of God in terms of His redemption of humankind, still made in His image, from the depravity it had fallen to.[2] The primary redemptive messenger will himself be human, a man ("seed"[3]). God's object will be to reach all peoples, and His

---

[2]That humanity retained the image of God even after the Fall is stated in Gen. 5:3 and 9:6. Although the image is marred, it is still correct to refer to humankind as being created in God's image.

[3]Note the masculine singular pronoun "he" referring to the seed in Gen. 3:15.

envoys will themselves be those made in His image.

Second comes the destruction of the world through a flood, followed by a blessing upon the house of Shem (Gen. 6 to 9). In 9:26, Yahweh is called the " 'God [Heb. *Elohim*] of Shem.' " The house of Shem is thus set off in a special sense as a people of God. This theme expands in 9:27, where it is stated that "God shall enlarge Japheth, and he shall dwell in the tents of Shem; and Canaan shall be his servant" (KJV). The NIV interprets the antecedent of the pronoun "he" to be Japheth, inferring that Japheth would share in the blessings already promised Shem.[4] Walter C. Kaiser sees in Genesis 9:27 an identification of this blessing in terms of the presence of God dwelling within the tents of Shem. This view holds the antecedent of the pronoun to be God, not Japheth. It is this special dwelling of God that becomes the means of His blessing.[5] In either view, God gives a blessing through the house of Shem as a projection of hope for all people following the judgment of the flood.

Third follows the judgment of human arrogance at Babel (Gen. 11:1–9), followed by God's promise to bless all peoples on earth through Abraham: "The Lord had said to Abram, 'Leave your country, your people and your father's household and go to the land I will show you. I will make you into a great nation and I will bless you; I will make your name great, and you will be a blessing. I will bless those who bless you, and whoever curses you I will curse; and all peoples on earth will be blessed through you.' " (Gen. 12:1–3)

The table of seventy representative nations had previously been listed in Genesis 10 as background to this promise to bless all nations. In Genesis 11:4, the inhabitants of Babel said, " 'Come, let us build ourselves a

---

[4]John H. Sailhamer, "Genesis," in *The Expositor's Bible Commentary*, ed. Frank E. Gaebelein (Grand Rapids: Zondervan Publishing House, 1990), 2:97.

[5]Kaiser, *Old Testament Theology*, 80–82.

city, with a tower that reaches to the heavens, so that we may make a name for ourselves and not be scattered over the face of the whole earth.' " Their desire to " 'make a name' " for themselves was opposed to the reign of God. The judgment that followed included the scattering of the peoples throughout the earth. This set the stage for the great declaration of Genesis 12:3 that through Abraham " 'all peoples' " (" 'nations,' " TEV) would be blessed.

Unveiling the promise to bless all nations, God clarifies His mission as being the fiery center for the rest of Scripture. God will move redemptively to establish His kingdom in which all nations will be blessed through the promised seed. Genesis 1 to 12, therefore, provides the foundational statement of the *missio Dei,* thereafter developed diachronically throughout the remainder of both Old and New Testaments.

MISSIO DEI: FURTHER DEVELOPMENT

The last line of the promise of blessing to Abraham (Gen. 12:3) should be regarded as the blessing's apex and controlling motif: " *'And all peoples on earth will be blessed through you.' "*[6] The blessing is cumulative in the sense of adding provisions until the whole is great enough to accomplish the blessing of the nations. As Kaiser observes: "Indeed, world-wide blessing was the whole purpose of the very first statement of the promise in 12:3."[7] Subsequent promises, such as that of land (13:15) and an heir (15:4), are likewise the means through which the promise to bless the nations is to be achieved.

The certainty of God's promise plan is emphasized in Genesis 15:9–21. When Abraham wondered how he could be sure of the promises of an heir and land, God

---

[6]Ibid., 86; Sailhamer, "Genesis," 110.
[7]Kaiser, *Old Testament Theology,* 86; see also Sailhamer, "Genesis," 111–12.

responded by making[8] a covenant with Abraham (v. 18). In this theophany, "a smoking firepot with a blazing torch" passed between the pieces of slaughtered animals arranged by Abraham (v. 17). Symbolically, God was pledging His life as a guarantee of His word. Though seed and land are the immediate context of this covenant, the wider context is the entire promise given to Abraham, especially the promise to bless all nations (12:3). In the words of Walter Kaiser, "Such a material or temporal blessing was not to be torn apart from the spiritual aspect of God's great promise."[9] The promise to bless all nations is emphasized both by its position as the final and therefore summary promise in 12:2–3 and by its repetition, first to Abraham (Gen. 18:18, 22:18) and then to both Isaac (26:4) and Jacob (28:14). It is noteworthy that in 22:18, 26:4, and 28:14, the promise is accompanied by the specific proviso that the blessing of the nations is to be accomplished through Abraham's seed.

The promise of the seed of the woman (3:15) thus anticipates the promise to Abraham, Isaac, and Jacob of a seed through whom all nations will be blessed. It is in this framework of a promised seed of blessing that the house of Judah is assigned the leading role (49:10) and later David, from the house of Judah, is promised an eternal Kingdom (2 Sam. 7, especially v. 16).

The New Testament begins by pointing out that Jesus is "the son of David, the son of Abraham" (Matt. 1:1), identifying Him both as the heir of the promised eternal Kingdom and as the promised seed of blessing to the nations. This is the historical clarification necessary for understanding the dual Great Commission themes of *kingdom authority* and *all nations* (Matt. 28:18–20).

Since God's mission has always been to all nations, it is not surprising to find numerous other direct and

---

[8]The Heb. has "the Lord *cut* a covenant," since a sacrifice was involved.
[9]Kaiser, *Old Testament Theology*, 90.

indirect references to God's love for the nations within the history of Israel. A few examples follow.

COVENANT WITNESS

One function of the Law given through Moses is to favorably demonstrate life in *the fear of the Lord* (more fully discussed in chapter 2). This distinctive way of life was a means of instructing the nations. The entire covenant at Sinai should be understood as a treaty deliberately enacted according to the prevailing treaty format of the day: a sovereign king entering into a covenant with a vassal. This format included (1) an identification of parties to the covenant, (2) a review of the history leading to the covenant, (3) statements of general and specific covenant provisions, (4) a public reading and depositing of the terms of the covenant, (5) the presence of witnesses (typically witnessing "deities"), and (6) a statement of blessings for covenant compliance and cursings for covenant noncompliance.[10] These six features are all given in Exodus 20:1 to 23:33. Besides satisfying the need for a formal statement of greater (Exod. 20:3–17) and lesser commands (Exod. 20:22 to 23:13), the Law was given to describe the lifestyle of a people bound by covenant to Yahweh. The reasonableness, justice, and protection offered under this law were intended to recommend and invite participation by the nations not yet in covenant.

A KINGDOM OF PRIESTS

This witnessing aspect of the covenant is shown in Exodus 19:5–6 with a statement that echoes throughout the rest of Scripture. God affirms that, though the whole world is His, Israel through obedience could become His " 'treasured possession,' " " 'a kingdom of priests and a holy nation.' " God's intention to bless the

---

[10]Merrill, "Theology of the Pentateuch," 33–35.

nations had long been known. Priestly service involves serving as an intermediary both through proclamation and intercession. Since holiness necessarily involves separation to the purpose of God, it follows that God was revealing His will that Israel bless the nations by both proclaiming His covenant to them and interceding on their behalf.

Centuries later, the echoes of this verse are found in the New Testament writings of Paul, Peter, and John. Paul referred to the grace God gave him "to be a minister of Christ Jesus to the Gentiles with the priestly duty of proclaiming the gospel of God, so that the Gentiles might become an offering acceptable to God, sanctified by the Holy Spirit" (Rom. 15:16). Similarly, Peter saw the new people of God, primarily Gentile, as "a chosen people, a royal priesthood, a holy nation, a people belonging to God, that [they might] declare the praises of him who called [them] out of darkness into his wonderful light" (1 Pet. 2:9). This separated life, Peter assured his readers, would mean that others will "see [their] good deeds and glorify God" (1 Pet. 2:12). John also wrote to the churches of his day using the words of Exodus 19:6: "[Christ] made us to be a kingdom and priests to serve his God and Father" (Rev. 1:6). Similar verses occur in Revelation 5:10 and 20:6.

SHEMA

The famed *Shema* text (Deut. 6:4–5) insists upon the unity of God. "Hear, O Israel. The Lord our God, the Lord is one" (v. 4). This is entirely consistent with the self-revelation of God in the creation chapters of Genesis and, like those chapters, implies a future mission to all nations. God, having the character that He does and being the only God, can never rest until all His creation is made to recognize and submit to His kingship.

TRIPARTITE FORMULA

By "tripartite formula" I mean the phrase "I will be your God, you will be my people, and I will dwell in the midst of you." The beginnings of this phrase first appear in Genesis 17:7–8; and it appears repeatedly, in whole or in part, throughout first the Old and then the New Testament. Walter Kaiser states: "This formula became the great hallmark of all biblical theology in both testaments."[11] The desire of God to have a people who serve him in covenant faithfulness is at the heart of *missio Dei.* That the divine objective is finally achieved is seen in Revelation 21:3: "I heard a loud voice from the throne saying, 'Now the dwelling of God is with men, and he will live with them. They will be his people, and God himself will be with them and be their God.'"

SPIRIT OF PROPHECY

In an interesting historical note recorded in Numbers 11:26–29, two elders, Eldad and Medad, prophesied as the Spirit rested upon them "in the camp" (v. 26) rather than around the Tent of Meeting with the rest of the seventy, where the Spirit had come upon them for that purpose (v. 16). But Moses refused to rebuke the prophetic manifestation of the two. Instead, seemingly anticipating the great day later prophesied by Joel, Moses said, " 'I wish that all the Lord's people were prophets and that the Lord would put His Spirit on them' " (11:29). Later this would take place as God's chosen means for accomplishing His mission.

KINGDOM PROMISES

God made significant promises when He changed Abram's name to Abraham in Genesis 17:1–8, including the promise that kings would come from him. Though

---

[11]Kaiser, *Old Testament Theology,* 33.

these kings would include the leaders of the " 'nations' " coming from Abraham, they would also include the line of kings ordained by God to rule over Israel. John H. Sailhamer explains the phrase " 'kings will come from you' " (17:6b) as follows: "It provides a link between the general promise of blessing through the seed of Abraham and the author's subsequent focus of that blessing in the royal house of Judah (Gen. 49:8–12; Num. 24:7–9). . . . At work here is the same theological planning as that lying behind the structure of the genealogy of Matthew 1: 'A record of the genealogy of Jesus Christ the son of David, the son of Abraham.' Keeping in mind the close association of the term 'messiah' *(christos)* with the kingship elsewhere in biblical literature (e.g., 1 Sam. 24:6, 10), it is not too far from the truth to speak of a 'Christology' of Genesis in such passages."[12]

God later gave Jacob a similar revelation, specifically including the provision that he would be a father of kings (Gen. 35:11).

That God's promise plan to bless the nations would involve a kingdom is explicitly stated in at least three other passages within the Pentateuch. The first of such passages is Genesis 49:10: " 'The scepter will not depart from Judah, nor the ruler's staff from between his feet, until he comes to whom it belongs and the obedience of the nations is his.' " It is particularly significant in the light of later Scriptures that this verse both anticipates Judah as the ruling tribe and the Kingdom as encompassing the nations. Though the "bless the nations" theme was well known by this time, the reader should see as an addition to the promise plan the specification of Judah as the ruling tribe through whom the blessing would be mediated.

The second is the account of Balaam (Num. 22 to 24), which gives a further prophetic explanation of Israel's role as a theocracy and of the Lord's kingly function.

---

[12]Sailhamer, "Genesis," 139.

Though Balaam was a pagan soothsayer (Josh. 13:22), the Lord's self-disclosure to him and the oracles he delivered are remarkable for their insight into God's blessing upon Israel. This is especially significant in the light of the function of the blessing and cursing provisions of the Abrahamic covenant. As has been seen above, Abraham was blessed that he might bless all nations. Had Balaam succeeded in cursing Israel, the nations would not have had the blessing of revelation even then being mediated to them through Israel, nor would they have had the hope of sharing in the blessing promised through the seed of Abraham, the Messiah. So in the attempt to hire Balaam, Balak king of Moab was challenging, albeit unwittingly, the entire promise plan of God.

The issue at stake was God's role as Sovereign of both Israel and the rest of the nations. Though God had said He had the power to bless and curse (Gen. 12:3), Balak attributed this power to Balaam (Num. 22:6). Balaam's reputation as a soothsayer depended upon his skill in manipulating the spirits. However, when he came face-to-face with the Sovereign Creator, he had far more than met his match. His inability to manipulate God is so complete and so elaborately developed as to be almost comic. Early on, God forbade Balaam to go with the first delegation from Moab, since Israel had been blessed and could not be cursed (Num. 22:12). When Balaam was later allowed to accompany a second delegation, that his real purpose was in keeping with Balak's request seems shown by the Lord's opposition along the road.[13] After the Lord "opened Balaam's eyes" (22:31), his journey took on a tone far different from that desired by Balak: Balaam consistently spoke words of blessing concerning Israel's future on behalf of the Lord, whose sovereignty is in

[13]Ronald B. Allen, "Numbers," in *The Expositor's Bible Commentary,* ed. Frank E. Gaebelein (Grand Rapids: Zondervan Publishing House, 1990), 2:889.

focus throughout the entire passage.

Several points emerge from Balaam's oracles that advance the theme of the Sovereign Lord's choice of Israel as a people of promise. In the first oracle, the blessing upon Israel is reaffirmed (Num. 23:8), Israel's unique destiny among the nations is mentioned (23:9), and Balaam's exclamation that he wanted a death " 'like theirs' " hints of the extension of grace to the nations (23:10). The second oracle focuses upon God, who is not a man that he should lie (23:19), who will fulfill His promises (23:19), who has pronounced blessing upon Israel (23:20), and who is personally the King dwelling among Israel (23:21). And, as Ronald B. Allen observes, "Since Yahweh the King is in their midst, they are invincible from outside attack."[14] Finally, Israel will devour its enemies because there is no sorcery against a people thus blessed by God (23:23–24).

The third oracle (Num. 23:27 to 24:14) once again refers to the general blessing upon Israel (24:5–7a) and the greatness of Israel's King (24:7b), especially with reference to hostile nations (24:8–9), including a citation from Genesis 12:3 of the results of blessing or cursing Israel.[15] The fourth oracle contains a remarkably clear messianic prophecy of a future star coming from Jacob, a scepter from Israel, and a ruler from Jacob— One who will completely defeat all enemies (24:15–19). The fifth, sixth, and seventh oracles prophesy ruin to those nations that would be hostile to Israel (24:20–24).

The third specific kingdom passage is the "law of the king" found in Deuteronomy 17:14–20. This passage so dramatically anticipates the future king that some have concluded it is from a much later period.[16] There is,

---

[14]Ibid., 902.

[15]The NASB has a note for Num. 24:9 to indicate that these words are believed to be from Gen. 12:3.

[16]For a discussion of this text, see J. A. Thompson, *Deuteronomy*, vol. 5 of *Tyndale Old Testament Commentaries*, ed. D. J. Wiseman (Downers Grove, Ill.: InterVarsity Press, 1974), 204–5.

however, no compelling reason to suspect this text, especially in the light of the *missio Dei* that we have been tracing. It was already known that the blessing of the nations would be associated with a ruler's scepter from Judah. Here God circumscribes the agency of kingdom in accomplishing His plan to ensure that the sovereign/vassal nature of His covenant would remain fixed—in contrast to the patterns of kingship common in Canaan.

Historical Books:
The Kingdom in *Missio Dei*

JOSHUA

Within the book of Joshua, the people in covenant with God move from a nomadic to a settled lifestyle in the Promised Land. This book demonstrates three major principles for a people in covenant with the God of mission.

The first is that God's manifest presence accompanies those who advance toward His kingdom according to His will. Within the book of Joshua, God's will is seen as possessing the Promised Land. This, in turn, is progress toward the establishment of the Kingdom already anticipated within the Pentateuch. In Deuteronomy 31, Moses had assured Joshua of the Lord's presence: " 'Do not be afraid or terrified because of them, for the Lord your God goes with you; he will never leave you nor forsake you. . . . The Lord himself goes before you and will be with you; he will never leave you nor forsake you.' " (vv. 6,8). After Moses' death, the Lord himself reaffirmed the promise: " 'No one will be able to stand up against you all the days of your life. As I was with Moses, so I will be with you; I will never leave you nor forsake you. . . . Have I not commanded you? Be strong and courageous. Do not be terrified; do not be discouraged, for the Lord your God will be with you wherever you go'" (Josh. 1:5,9).

Under Joshua, God's covenant people advanced bold-ly to accomplish the mission of their God and King; they moved in assurance that the manifest presence of God was among them. God's promise to Joshua would later provide the basic wording for Jesus' assurance to His disciples when He sent them on His mission: " 'There-fore go and make disciples of all nations, baptizing them in the name of the Father and of the Son and of the Holy Spirit, and teaching them to obey everything I have com-manded you. And surely I am with you always, to the very end of the age'" (Matt. 28:19–20).

In the same spirit Jesus had earlier assured his disci-ples: " 'I will not leave you as orphans; I will come to you'" (John 14:18). In any age, those called by God to accomplish His purpose are assured of His manifest presence.

The second principle illustrated in Joshua is that all true victories in the kingdom of God are done with the blessing of the nations in view. Twice in Joshua 3, God is referred to as "the Lord of all the earth": "See, the ark of the covenant of the Lord of all the earth will go into the Jordan ahead of you. . . . And as soon as the priests who carry the ark of the Lord—the Lord of all the earth—set foot in the Jordan, its waters flowing downstream will be cut off and stand up in a heap" (vv. 11,13).

At first glance, it may seem ironic that a mission designed to bless the nations should begin with mili-tary conquest. But to accomplish this worldwide bless-ing, Israel needed a base of operation.

"Specifically, the conquest of Canaan under Joshua's leadership grew out of the Abrahamic Covenant. God, having dealt with all nations, made Abraham the cen-ter of His purposes and determined to reach the lost world through Abraham's seed."[17]

---

[17]John F. Walvoord and Roy B Zuck, *The Bible Knowledge Com-mentary* (Wheaton, Ill.: Scripture Press Publications, 1985), 326.

Since God made the world and is the "Lord of all the earth," the text assumes His right to allocate the land as He chooses. It should be further noted that the conquest of Canaan is portrayed in Scripture as a punishment of societies that had become ripe for judgment; the land had been spoken of as having " 'vomited out' " its inhabitants (Lev. 18:28). Israel's conquests were undertaken with inferior equipment, most notably the lack of chariots, yet they won due to the Lord's presence. Further, Israel was warned that if they did not remain obedient to the covenant with Yahweh, they too would be vomited out—a fate later fulfilled through the Assyrian and Babylonian captivities (Lev. 18:28; 20:22).

Joshua 3:11–13 announces that the ark of the covenant of the Lord of all the earth would go into the Jordan River ahead of them. These verses should be viewed as setting a spiritual foundation for the conquest that follows and for the later development of the theme of God's lordship over all the earth. It is as the nations submit to God's lordship that they will be blessed. Later references to "the Lord of all the earth" or parallel references include the following:

- The earth is the Lord's, and everything in it, the world, and all who live in it (Ps. 24:1).
- "For your Maker is your husband—the Lord Almighty is his name—the Holy One of Israel is your Redeemer; he is called the God of all the earth" (Isa. 54:5).
- Who should not revere you, O King of the nations? This is your due. Among all the wise men of the nations and in all their kingdoms, there is no one like you (Jer. 10:7).
- "Rise and thresh, O Daughter of Zion, for I will give you horns of iron; I will give you hoofs of bronze and you will break to pieces many nations." You will devote their ill-gotten gains to the LORD, their wealth to the Lord of all the earth (Mic. 4:13).

- The Lord will be awesome to them when he destroys all the gods of the land. The nations on every shore will worship him, every one in its own land (Zeph. 2:11).
- So he said, "These are the two who are anointed to serve the Lord of all the earth" (Zech. 4:14).
- The angel answered me, "These are the four spirits of heaven, going out from standing in the presence of the Lord of the whole world" (Zech. 6:5).
- The Lord will be king over the whole earth. On that day there will be one Lord, and his name the only name (Zech. 14:9).

It is thus not surprising that the Book of Joshua affirms the following reason for the miraculous crossing of Israel over Jordan: " 'He did this so that all the peoples of the earth might know that the hand of the Lord is powerful' " (Josh. 4:24).

The third great principle relating to God's mission taught by Joshua is allocation. This concept is demonstrated in Joshua through the systematic apportionment of Canaan to the tribes of Israel. After the initial victories in the Central, Southern, and Northern campaigns (Josh. 6 to 12), there remained great areas to be taken over (Josh. 13:1). The general plan of allocation is stated in Joshua 13:6: " 'As for all the inhabitants of the mountain regions from Lebanon to Misrephoth Maim, that is, all the Sidonians, I myself will drive them out before the Israelites. Be sure to allocate this land to Israel for an inheritance, as I have instructed you.' " This instruction is, in turn, consistent with what Moses had commanded Joshua: "Then Moses summoned Joshua and said to him in the presence of all Israel, 'Be strong and courageous, for you must go with this people into the land that the Lord swore to their forefathers to give them, and you must divide it among them as their inheritance' " (Deut. 31:7).

After the text deals with Judah and the two Joseph tribes in Joshua 13 to 17, a more detailed instruction is given for the allocation procedure for the remaining tribes:

> So Joshua said to the Israelites: "How long will you wait before you begin to take possession of the land that the Lord, the God of your fathers, has given you? Appoint three men from each tribe. I will send them out to make a survey of the land and to write a description of it, according to the inheritance of each. Then they will return to me. You are to divide the land into seven parts. Judah is to remain in its territory on the south and the house of Joseph in its territory on the north. After you have written descriptions of the seven parts of the land, bring them here to me and I will cast lots for you in the presence of the Lord our God." . . .
>
> As the men started on their way to map out the land, Joshua instructed them, "Go and make a survey of the land and write a description of it. Then return to me, and I will cast lots for you here at Shiloh in the presence of the Lord." So the men left and went through the land. They wrote its description on a scroll, town by town, in seven parts, and returned to Joshua in the camp at Shiloh (Josh. 18:3–6,8–9).

With each statement of what had to be done came the directive that the task was to be divided into subtasks and allocated according to tribal division. It follows that when God specifies a task to be done by His people, He expects their leadership to identify the total task, divide it into components, and allocate them to identifiable systems and subsystems. Responsibility for its accomplishment may then be determined with reports to different levels of leadership. This principle is consistent with the foundational understanding that people are made in the image of God (Gen. 1:27) and are therefore capable of representing God. It is God's nature to entrust human beings, those He has created, with specified missions as means toward the accomplishment of His grand design for history.

The Lord had previously determined the nature and extent of the task, that is, the land to be taken. It was understood that membership in the people of God required participation in completing the assigned task. Full victory was expected regardless of the obstacles (Josh. 17:14–18). Though the present-day Church lacks the central authority of Israel at the time of the conquest of Canaan, groups of like-minded believers throughout the world have nonetheless committed themselves to an application of the principle of allocation with respect to reaching unreached peoples.

Though Western nations have often followed up their unreached people group research with appeals for volunteers to "adopt a people," other parts of the world are sometimes more open to simply assign responsibility for such unreached peoples, Joshua-style. In Nigeria, for example, the Assemblies of God have assigned unreached people groups to districts and churches with successful church planting then following.

JUDGES AND RUTH

In the books of Judges and Ruth, God's Kingdom is anticipated in such a way as to open it up for the Gentiles. The key line of Judges, " 'The Lord will rule over you' " (8:23), is central to its ascending and descending literary structure.[18] The plan of God is contrasted with the futility of life outside His Kingdom, serving to prepare the people for the divinely appointed Davidic vice-regents who will soon rule on behalf of the Lord. The power of the Holy Spirit is effective in maintaining a consciousness of God's Kingdom even through the most difficult times (Judg. 6:34).

In Ruth, the narrative looks toward the Davidic kingdom through the historical lens of a kinsman-redeemer acting on behalf of a Gentile woman. In a significant genealogy, the Book of Ruth ends by linking Perez the son of Judah with David (4:18–22). In this way, Judges

[18]Kenneth Barker, ed., *The NIV Study Bible* (Grand Rapids: Zondervan Publishing House, 1985), 327.

and Ruth are connected to both their Genesis antecedents and the Davidic kingdom that follows.

Davidic Kingdom

In a dramatic conversation between the Lord and David through Nathan, David offers to build a house (i.e., a temple) for God. After initially welcoming the idea, Nathan returns to David with a message from the Lord: David will not build a house for God, but rather God will build a house (i.e., a dynasty) for David (2 Sam. 7:11). Remarkably, God further states, " ' "Your house and your kingdom will endure forever before me; your throne will be established forever" ' "(2 Sam. 7:16).

David's response to this revelation is noteworthy: " 'Is this your usual way of dealing with man?' " (7:19). The key word in this passage, " 'usual way' " (Heb. *torah*), literally means "teaching" and is most often used in the sense of God's instruction or laws. In this case, David seems to use *torah* in the sense of a charter.[19] He links the new revelation of an eternal kingdom to God's previously revealed plan for the nations and concludes that such a Kingdom must indeed be the charter *(torah)* for all humankind (Heb. *'adam*). This eternal Kingdom conferred upon the house of David (2 Sam. 7:1–17, 1 Chron. 17:1–15) thus becomes the means of fulfilling the earlier prophetic expectations of the Pentateuch. God's kingdom, of necessity both eternal and universal, would henceforth be identified with the house of David.

Davidic kings were, therefore, vice-regents representing the great Sovereign Creator who had ordained that through Abraham would come both a seed and a kingdom of priests destined to bless all nations. Any attempt by Jews or their leaders to utilize the Kingdom for personal benefit was therefore unfaithfulness to the

---

[19]Kaiser, *Old Testament Theology,* 154–55.

great King and His purpose for the nations. This understanding of a kingdom of priests was the foundational concept to the subsequent historical books and was joyously celebrated in the Psalms. Life in the Kingdom was described in the Wisdom Literature, and the prophets held both king and people accountable for their compliance with the covenant.

STUDY QUESTIONS

1. What is the meaning of the term "diachronic"?
2. Within this study, what does the term *missio Dei* mean?
3. In what ways does the account of creation serve as the basis for a theology of missions?
4. Explain the two great missiological implications of the statement that humankind is made in God's image (Gen. 1:26–27).
5. Explain the progression of thought from Genesis 1 to 11 leading to the promise to bless all nations in Genesis 12:3.
6. In what sense were the covenant and law given in Exodus missiological?
7. Explain the missional signification of the following: A kingdom of priests, *Shema*, tripartite formula, Spirit of prophecy, kingdom promises.
8. From the Book of Joshua, explain the significance of three foundational principles of a people bound by covenant to the God of mission.
9. In 2 Samuel 7, God promises David an eternal kingdom. What function does this promise have within the Old Testament? How is it foundational to the New Testament?

Chapter 2:

Missio Dei in the Poetical Books and the Prophets: Celebration, Covenant Lawsuit, and New Beginnings

Poetical Books

The theme of *missio Dei* is strongly evident throughout the Wisdom Literature of the Old Testament. A variety of covenant terms, key words, and literary forms celebrate the idealized relationship between the Creator and His creation. It is this "life in the Kingdom" that was intended to draw the nations irresistibly into the covenant relationship with the one God of all the earth.

JOB

The presence of Job within the Jewish canon of Holy Scripture should be recognized as being missiologically significant. (1) There is a notable absence of reference to the Mosaic legal system, indicating a pre-Mosaic era. (2) The setting of Job is patriarchal, shown by such practices as the father's role as spiritual head of the family.[1]

---

[1] Roy B. Zuck, "A Theology of the Wisdom Books and the Song of Solomon," in *A Biblical Theology of the Old Testament*, ed. Roy B. Zuck (Chicago: Moody Press, 1989), 208; Walter C. Kaiser, *Toward an Old Testament Theology* (Grand Rapids: Zondervan Publishing House, 1978), 97.

During this pre-Mosaic period, God maintained a close relationship with those from families that were not ancestors of the nation of Israel. Key concepts from Job consistent with the rest of the Old Testament include a strong emphasis upon God as the universal Creator and Controller of history who holds human beings morally accountable both during their lifetime and at the future time of resurrection. This message is consistent with the later Jewish prophets who often indicated that the Creator God would once again be worshiped throughout the entire earth.

Psalms

In the Psalms, the universal rule of God is a strong theme—confirming that Israel understood the Pentateuch as teaching an inclusion of all nations in the blessing plan of God. It should be noted that royal psalms generally go beyond the reign of the ruling Davidic king to envision the glories of the messianic King. This association naturally leads to a consideration of the nations, which must of necessity be a part of the messianic kingdom. There is therefore a strong connection between royal psalms and the repeated references to the nations throughout the psalms.

Psalms with a specific theme of salvation for the nations include Psalms 2, 9, 18, 22, 33, 45, 46, 47, 48, 49, 57, 65, 67, 68, 72, 76, 77, 79, 82, 83, 86, 87, 94, 95, 96, 97, 98, 99, 100, 102, 103, 105, 108, 114, 117, 118, 126, 138, 139, 144, 145, 146, 150. Selections from this list are treated below.

> Why do the nations conspire and the peoples plot in vain? The kings of the earth take their stand and the rulers gather together against the Lord and against his Anointed One. "Let us break their chains," they say, "and throw off their fetters." The One enthroned in heaven laughs; the Lord scoffs at them. Then he rebukes them in his anger and terrifies them in his wrath, saying, "I have installed my King on Zion, my holy hill." I will proclaim the decree

The Poetical Books and the Prophets 43

of the Lord: He said to me, "You are my Son; today I have
become your Father. Ask of me, and I will make the
nations your inheritance, the ends of the earth your possession. You will rule them with an iron scepter; you will
dash them to pieces like pottery." Therefore, you kings, be
wise; be warned, you rulers of the earth. Serve the Lord
with fear and rejoice with trembling. Kiss the Son, lest he
be angry and you be destroyed in your way, for his wrath
can flare up in a moment. Blessed are all who take refuge
in him (Ps. 2:1–12).

Psalm 2 is typical of many royal psalms in that it celebrates the rule of a divinely appointed King over the
whole earth. It is a coronation psalm, in which the
newly crowned king is invited to request the nations as
his inheritance, the ends of the earth as his possession.
That this psalm is messianic is shown by the contrast
between the magnitude of the Kingdom it celebrates
(the whole world) and the divine limitations placed
upon the size of the nation of Israel (Gen. 15:18–21;
Deut. 1:7; 11:24; 34:1–4; Josh. 1:4).

It may possibly have been an inclination to ignore
this territorial restriction which led to David's punishment in the matter of numbering the people (2 Sam.
24:11–17). The taking of a census usually indicated an
impending military campaign involving conscription
and additional taxation. If, as appears to be the case, the
extent of David's rule had been already realized, then
his census-taking could indicate an unauthorized
intent to expand beyond God's boundaries—an offense
of extreme gravity. It is also possible to see David's
offense as taking pride in the size to which the kingdom
had grown.

In either case, what sense can be made of Psalm 2 and
the many like it that celebrate a worldwide extension of
the kingdom? Some simply dismiss these psalms as the
hyperbole of exuberant nationalists. But interpreting
them in the light of the antecedent theology of the
Pentateuch is much preferred. Far from sharing in an
unholy pride or ethnic nationalism, the Psalmists were

prophets who foresaw the day already announced when all nations would be blessed through the promised seed of Abraham. Further, the Psalmists were also aware of the eternal nature of David's kingdom. This is shown by Psalm 89, in which the Psalmist held the apparent demise of the Davidic kingdom during the Babylonian exile as being inconsistent with the promise to David of an eternal kingdom.

While we may be puzzled by the seeming conflict between the geographical limitations placed upon the kingdom in the Pentateuch and the worldwide kingdom envisioned in the Psalms, the Psalmists do not seem to be overly concerned about any such supposed problem. In the grip of the same prophetic Spirit who had spoken to Abraham, they celebrated a kingdom that was both eternal and universal.

Of course, when we come to the New Testament, the problem is easily solved. The "Son" (Ps. 2:7) is neither David nor any of his immediate successors. Rather, the Son is Jesus, whose eternal sonship is declared through His resurrection from the dead (Acts 13:33). It is important to note that Jesus' sonship did not begin at the Incarnation, as some have supposed from reading these verses. Rather, the quotation of Psalm 2:7 in Acts 13:33 would indicate that the Resurrection was equivalent to an inauguration. The public proclamation to all nations of Jesus' eternal sonship begins with His resurrection from the dead. Derek Kidner writes of Psalm 2:7–9: "Our Lord's post-resurrection charges to the apostles emphasized *the nations* and *the ends of the earth,* pointedly taking up this promise to the newly authenticated king. It has continued to launch missionary ventures whenever its force has come home to the church."[2]

---

[2]Derek Kidner, *Psalms 1–72*, vol. 14a of *Tyndale Old Testament Commentaries*, ed. D. J. Wiseman (Downers Grove, Ill.: InterVarsity Press, 1973), 51, Kidner's emphasis.

> There is a river whose streams make glad the city of
> God, the holy place where the Most High dwells. God is
> within her, she will not fall; God will help her at break of
> day. Nations are in uproar, kingdoms fall; he lifts his voice,
> the earth melts. The Lord Almighty is with us; the God of
> Jacob is our fortress. (Ps. 46:4–7).

Then comes the admonition of Psalm 46:10, " 'Be still,
and know that I am God; I will be exalted among the
nations, I will be exalted in the earth.' " This psalm
shows God to be in control despite uncertainties that
seem to have included a serious threat to the security
and peace of Jerusalem. Verse 7 was the basis of Martin
Luther's famous hymn "A Mighty Fortress." The key
thought is that the security of Jerusalem leads to the
exaltation of God among the nations of the earth. Given
the antecedent Scriptures, that exaltation among the
nations is to be equated with their being blessed and
includes every sense in which God rules them. The fact
that Jerusalem was the God-ordained center of worship
for God's covenant people was not to imply that He
ruled only Israel. To the contrary, through both peaceful and hostile contact with the nations, Israel's worldview was to be expanded so that they would understand God's kingdom to be over all the earth. The
phrase " 'Be still' " could be translated "Stop" or
"Enough." The people's vision for a secure Jerusalem
was too small. Rather, God's fatherly protection of
Israel was to showcase the fear of the Lord as living
within Israel until the Lord's exaltation in all the earth.

> Clap your hands, all you nations; shout to God with
> cries of joy. How awesome is the Lord Most High, the great
> King over all the earth! He subdued nations under us, peo-
> ples under our feet. He chose our inheritance for us, the
> pride of Jacob, whom he loved. God has ascended amid
> shouts of joy, the Lord amid the sounding of trumpets.
> Sing praises to God, sing praises; sing praises to our King,
> sing praises. For God is the King of all the earth; sing to
> him a psalm of praise. God reigns over the nations; God is
> seated on his holy throne. The nobles of the nations assem-

ble as the people of the God of Abraham, for the kings of
the earth belong to God; he is greatly exalted (Ps. 47:1–9).

Psalm 47 celebrates the crowning of a Davidic king
by boldly including all the nations in the blessing
implied by the Abrahamic covenant (vv. 7–9). As noted
earlier, this twin theme of *kingdom* and *nations* is carried
into the New Testament. Matthew links Jesus with
David (kingdom) and Abraham (nations) in the beginning of his Gospel (1:1) to foreshadow the climax of his
Gospel, where kingdom (i.e., " 'authority' ") is once again
linked with " 'nations' " (28:18–19).

Derek Kidner's comments on this psalm are especially helpful:

> Now, with a single word, the real end in view comes
> into sight. The innumerable *princes* and *peoples* are to
> become one *people;* and they will no longer be outsiders
> but within the covenant; this is implied in their being
> called *the people of the God of Abraham.* It is the abundant
> fulfillment of the promise of Genesis 12:3; it anticipates
> what Paul expounds of the inclusion of the Gentiles as
> Abraham's sons (Rom. 4:11; Gal. 3:7–9).
>
> But characteristically the psalm relates this to its theme,
> the kingly glory of God. Its comment is not "the nations
> will be at peace", true though it would be, but instead, *he
> is highly exalted. . . .* Meanwhile the gospel will reveal the
> unexpected kind of "exaltation" which will begin the
> process of "gathering" the peoples: "I, when I am lifted up
> . . . , will draw all men to myself" (John 12:32).[3]

Psalm 67 interprets the Aaronic benediction of
Numbers 6:24–26 as being for the salvation of the
nations. Israel was blessed to be a blessing to the
nations who, in their own turn, join Israel in joyful celebration of praise to God.

> May God be gracious to us and bless us and make his
> face shine upon us, that your ways may be known on
> earth, your salvation among all nations. May the peoples
> praise you, O God; may all the peoples praise you. May

---

[3]Ibid., 178, Kidner's emphasis.

the nations be glad and sing for joy, for you rule the peoples justly and guide the nations of the earth. May the peoples praise you, O God; may all the peoples praise you. Then the land will yield its harvest, and God, our God, will bless us. God will bless us, and all the ends of the earth will fear him (Ps. 67:1–7).

It should be noted that psalms such as this one serve as a window on the intent of the Pentateuch. God's plans known in the Pentateuch were interpreted and celebrated through the Psalms within the liturgical calendar of Israel. As is shown by this psalm, God's plan was understood to be the blessing of the nations through Israel.

It was as Israel violated the first three commandments by having other gods, making images for worship, and misusing the name of the Lord that it abandoned the worldview of the Pentateuch and adopted the limited worldview of its pagan neighbors. In both Psalm 115:8 and 135:18 the heathen are blamed for becoming like the idols they served. Hosea 4:7 speaks of Israel exchanging " 'their Glory for something disgraceful,' " meaning an idol. In Hosea 9:10, the sin of Israel in the time of Numbers is spoken of as their becoming " 'as vile as the thing they loved.' " Only as Israel held a high view of God, such as is taught in the Pentateuch and Psalms, did it maintain any sense of its destiny, as portrayed in Psalm 67, of radiating God's glory among the nations. Psalm 67 is one of the primary references in specifying the focus upon the nations that was foundational to Israel's faith.

He has set his foundation on the holy mountain; the Lord loves the gates of Zion more than all the dwellings of Jacob. Glorious things are said of you, O city of God: *Selah* "I will record Rahab and Babylon among those who acknowledge me—Philistia too, and Tyre, along with Cush—and will say, 'This one was born in Zion.' " Indeed, of Zion it will be said, "This one and that one were born in her, and the Most High himself will establish her." The Lord will write in the register of the peoples: "This one

was born in Zion." *Selah* As they make music they will
sing, "All my fountains are in you" (Ps. 87:1–7).

In the light of antecedent Scripture, it would be difficult to differ from the traditional Christian interpretation
of these verses such as that given by Derek Kidner: "A
representative sample of the Gentile world is being
enrolled in God's city. . . . Towards God, they are counted as *those who know me*, an even higher designation than
'those who fear me' (cf. Jer. 31:34). Towards the people of
God they are not mere proselytes: they can avow, as Paul
said of his Roman status, 'But I was born a citizen' (*cf.*
Acts 22:28). This is the gospel age, no less. . . . Here [v. 6]
is His 'book of life', written with His own hand (cf. The
right of entry into the city, into which the kings of the
earth bring their glory, in Rev. 21:24–27)."[4]

> Shout for joy to the Lord, all the earth. Worship the Lord
> with gladness; come before him with joyful songs. Know
> that the Lord is God. It is he who made us, and we are his;
> we are his people, the sheep of his pasture. Enter his gates
> with thanksgiving and his courts with praise; give thanks
> to him and praise his name. For the Lord is good and his
> love endures forever; his faithfulness continues through
> all generations (Ps. 100:1–5).

Psalms 93 to 100 are grouped by the common theme
of God's righteous rule over the nations. Though the
language of Psalm 100 describes the worship of Israel,
the call to worship extends to "all the earth" (v. 1). It is
all the earth that is to shout for joy and worship the
Lord with gladness in recognition that the Lord is God,
their creator (Ps. 24:1). It is this shout of acknowledge-
ment of the kingship of the Lord that stands as the single requirement to enter into the worship of Yahweh,
an anticipation of the New Testament teaching of justification by faith.

---

[4]Derek Kidner, *Psalms 73–150*, vol. 14b of *Tyndale Old Testament
Commentaries*, ed. D. J. Wiseman (Downers Grove, Ill.: InterVarsity
Press, 1973), 315, Kidner's emphasis.

"The joyful noise is not the special contribution of the tone-deaf, still less of the convivial, but the equivalent in worship to the homage-shout or fanfare (Ps. 98:6) for a king, as in 95:1 or the almost identical 66:1. This word claims the world for God."[5]

In Psalm 100, all the earth is under divine summons to worship, since worship is associated with creation (v. 3). The major verbs are parallel ("shout," "worship," "come," "know," "enter," "give thanks," and "praise"). It is all the worshiping earth, therefore, who are called the sheep of His pasture, who are invited to enter His gates with thanksgiving and His courts with praise, and who will enjoy the goodness of the Lord's eternal love. Of verse 4, Kidner comments: "The simplicity of this invitation may conceal the wonder of it, for the *courts* are truly *his,* not ours (as Is. 1:12 had to remind the triflers), and His *gates* are shut to the unclean (Rev. 21:27). Yet not only His outer courts but the Holy of Holies itself are thrown open 'by the new and living way', and we are welcome."[6]

> Praise the Lord, all you nations; extol him, all you peoples. For great is his love toward us, and the faithfulness of the Lord endures forever. Praise the Lord (Ps. 117:1–2).

Psalm 117 is of special significance, for the nations (Heb. *goyim*) are commanded to praise *Yahweh,* the covenant name that Israel used for God. In this brief Psalm, "us" must either refer to all the nations who are urged to praise the Lord or to the people of Israel whose life under the covenant serves to invite others to covenant fellowship. In either case, the psalm is clearly nations-oriented. In Romans 15:8–11, Paul chooses Psalm 117 as one of the Old Testament texts that most clearly summarizes the promise that the Gentiles (or nations) will be blessed through Israel: "For I tell you

[5]Ibid., 356.
[6]Ibid., 357, Kidner's emphasis.

that Christ has become a servant of the Jews on behalf of God's truth, to confirm the promises made to the patriarchs so that the Gentiles may glorify God for his mercy, as it is written: 'Therefore I will praise you among the Gentiles; I will sing hymns to your name.' . . . And again, 'Praise the Lord, all you Gentiles, and sing praises to him, all you peoples.'"

> The stone the builders rejected has become the capstone; the Lord has done this, and it is marvelous in our eyes. This is the day the Lord has made; let us rejoice and be glad in it. O Lord, save us; O Lord, grant us success. Blessed is he who comes in the name of the Lord. From the house of the Lord we bless you. The Lord is God, and he has made his light shine upon us. With boughs in hand, join in the festal procession up to the horns of the altar. You are my God, and I will give you thanks; you are my God, and I will exalt you. Give thanks to the Lord, for he is good; his love endures forever (Ps. 118:22–29).

Psalm 118:22–29 is a unit serving as an announcement and celebration of a future day the Lord will make for the accomplishment of His redemptive purposes. While this psalm's liturgical usage celebrated the blessing known through ruling Davidic kings, the focus is clearly future and messianic. That this was not missed by New Testament writers is shown by such references as Matthew 21:42; Mark 12:10–11; Luke 20:17; Acts 4:11; Ephesians 2:20; and 1 Peter 2:7.

The organizing verse of this section is verse 24, "This is the day the Lord has made; let us rejoice and be glad in it." This "day" begins with the rejection of Christ ("the stone the builders rejected," v. 22). Then the day moves to the cry *hosanna* ("O Lord, save us," v. 25), which literally means "save please!" or "save now!" and is followed by a prayer for success. Finally, the day concludes with the declaration of victory inherent in the words "Blessed is he who comes in the name of the Lord" (v. 26). Though these words were used at the triumphal entry (Matt. 21:9), Christ later identified their fuller meaning as referring to the time of His second coming

(Matt. 23:39). The day the Lord made, therefore, includes the cross, the time for success in the proclamation of redemption, and the return of the triumphant Lord.

It is especially significant that the cry *hosanna* is followed by the intercessory appeal, "O Lord, grant us success" (v. 25). Throughout the day the Lord made, from crucifixion to Second Coming, the praising covenant community announces salvation as it intercedes for success in fulfilling the mission of God.

Indeed, the Psalms celebrate the completion of *missio Dei,* God's mission to have a redeemed people from among all nations.

PROVERBS

The function of proverbs within the society of the ancients, as well as their content, cause them to stand out as beacons so that those from among all nations might find the pathway of wisdom. The account of Solomon demonstrates how wise men were sought out and their wisdom tested by visitors from afar. This common feature of ancient society took on a new dimension when those sharing wisdom walked in the fear of the Lord. In this case, the wisdom they shared contained the quality of witness appropriate to the divinely given destiny of the covenant people. In fact, the exchange of wisdom was one of the most acceptable ways for Israel to interact with the nations they were to bless.

The life of wisdom lived in the fear of the Lord provided a universal offer of instruction; by its very nature, wisdom is transcultural. Since the Israelites believed they served the Creator of all things, their truth claims were exclusive. Other religions served worthless idols. The Wisdom Literature provided at once the message of life, the invitation to that message, and the common cultural form whereby that message might be communicated.

The concept of the fear of the Lord might well be considered as the essential aspect of Israel's faith most characteristic of their life and witness. It is a recurrent theme in the Book of Proverbs, addressing respect for the name of the Lord, for the law ("instruction") of the Lord, and for the manner of life pleasing to the Lord. Each of the subjects treated within Proverbs in one way or another contributes to an understanding of how to live life in the fear of the Lord.

ECCLESIASTES

The significance of Ecclesiastes to *missio Dei* is found both in its contrast between the meaninglessness of life on one hand and the fear of the Lord on the other, and also in its form as Wisdom Literature. The book is set as the instruction of *Koheleth*, the teacher (master) of the assembly. It is by nature that type of instruction offered to all peoples: Those near and far are invited to consider the futility of life, however nobly lived, apart from the fear of the Lord. A remarkable concept is expressed in 3:11,14: "He has made everything beautiful in its time. He has also set eternity in the hearts of men; yet they cannot fathom what God has done from beginning to end. . . . I know that everything God does will endure forever; nothing can be added to it and nothing taken from it. God does it so that men will revere him."

These verses contrast with the well-known words opening the chapter, that there is "a time for everything" (3:1). As the *Full Life Study Bible* comments, "God has placed within the human heart an inherent desire for more than just the earthly. . . . Consequently, material things, secular activities, and the pleasures of this earth will never fully satisfy."[7] This sense of eternity is to be equated with the image of God in which humanity is created, thus making it an inborn concept common to all.

---

[7]Donald C. Stamps, ed., *The Full Life Study Bible* (Grand Rapids: Zondervan Publishing House, 1992), 949.

SONG OF SOLOMON

There are at least three ways the Song of Solomon may be viewed as contributing to *missio Dei*. First, it offers the protection of God's blessing within the marriage relationships of the covenant community, eliminating the sense of void that leads to sexual temptation. Second, it offers a statement of witness to the outside world of the strength and beauty of married love within God's covenant so as to demonstrate the inferiority of the pseudo-love typical of such traditions as those of Baal worship. Third, since from the most ancient of times this book has been interpreted allegorically, its idealized statement of human love may be said to bear witness to the nations by describing the love relationship between the Lord and His covenant people.

The God who created life offers a sacred glimpse into the most intimate of relationships so as to provide a sense of God-blessed mutual commitment that would safeguard the covenant community against illicit sexual conduct, bear witness to their neighbors of what it means to be blessed by God, and demonstrate God's love for His covenant people.

Prophets

The Old Testament prophets advanced the theme of *missio Dei* in three major ways: First, they brought something of a covenant lawsuit against the people of God. In doing this, they often looked beyond the immediate warning of judgment to see a time of restoration. This time of restoration often specifically included the blessing of the nations.

Second, the Old Testament prophets viewed the rule of God as encompassing all the earth. The nations are accountable to the moral Judge of the universe even though they had not participated in the historic covenants of the people of Israel. The prophets make repeated references to the judgment of God upon all nations, Gentile as well as Jewish.

Third, the prophets foretold the day of a new covenant. Under this new covenant, the blessings of restoration (spoken of above) would take place. In this new day, God's gracious Spirit would be poured out upon all peoples, resulting in salvation and leading to the eschatological day when all would live in harmony under the kingdom rule of God.

COVENANT LAWSUIT

A major function of the prophets was to hold the Israelites—royalty, religious leaders, everyone— accountable before God for their covenant responsibilities. Each covenant had its obligations before God. But the major point of reference for the prophets was the written law (Heb. *torah*), stating the responsibilities of the people under terms of the Sinaitic covenant. One of the means for stating God's case against Israel is in the form of a covenant lawsuit (Heb. *riv*). The Book of Micah is a specific example. Consider especially 6:1–2, in which the Lord brings His case against Israel before the mountains: "Listen to what the Lord says: 'Stand up, plead your case before the mountains; let the hills hear what you have to say. Hear, O mountains, the Lord's accusation; listen, you everlasting foundations of the earth. For the Lord has a case against his people; he is lodging a charge against Israel.' "

A summary of Israel's history is then presented to establish guilt, and Israel is required to remember specific events. With guilt established, Israel is pictured as offering various appeasements, only to hear that God's interest is in their doing justly, loving mercy, and walking humbly with Him (6:1–16).

JUDGMENT UPON ALL NATIONS

God judged Israel because they violated specific obligations of His covenant. Did all other nations' lack of such a covenantal history exclude them from God's moral rule and hence His judgment? Not according to the prophets. To the contrary, every nation was held accountable for its own violations of God's moral rule. That God's prophetic word would judge all the nations was explained to Jeremiah as follows:

> This is what the Lord, the God of Israel, said to me: "Take from my hand this cup filled with the wine of my wrath and make all the nations to whom I send you drink it. When they drink it, they will stagger and go mad because of the sword I will send among them."
>
> So I took the cup from the Lord's hand and made all the nations to whom he sent me drink it: Jerusalem and the towns of Judah, its kings and officials, to make them a ruin and an object of horror and scorn and cursing, as they are today; Pharaoh king of Egypt, his attendants, his officials and all his people, and all the foreign people there; all the kings of Uz; all the kings of the Philistines (those of Ashkelon, Gaza, Ekron, and the people left at Ashdod); Edom, Moab and Ammon; all the kings of Tyre and Sidon; the kings of the coastlands across the sea; Dedan, Tema, Buz and all who are in distant places; all the kings of Arabia and all the kings of the foreign people who live in the desert; all the kings of Zimri, Elam and Media; and all the kings of the north, near and far, one after the other—all the kingdoms on the face of the earth. And after all of them, the king of Sheshach will drink it too.
>
> . . .
>
> "Now prophesy all these words against them and say to them: 'The Lord will roar from on high; he will thunder from his holy dwelling and roar mightily against his land. He will shout like those who tread the grapes, shout against all who live on the earth. The tumult will resound to the ends of the earth, for the Lord will bring charges against the nations; he will bring judgment on all mankind and put the wicked to the sword,'" declares the Lord (Jer. 25:15–26,30–31).

Since no court may rule beyond its jurisdiction, these legal indictments are first a statement of God's universal rule and then an appeal to His covenant people to warn these nations of their impending doom so as to give them opportunity to repent. Isaiah's prophecies of judgment against the nations include 10:5–19; 13; 14:4–32; 16:6 to 21:17; 23; 24; 31; and 34. With a mounting cadence, Isaiah 24:1–6 explains the fact of international accountability to the justice of God as follows:

> See, the Lord is going to lay waste the earth and devastate it; he will ruin its face and scatter its inhabitants—it will be the same for priest as for people, for master as for servant, for mistress as for maid, for seller as for buyer, for borrower as for lender, for debtor as for creditor. The earth will be completely laid waste and totally plundered. The Lord has spoken this word. The earth dries up and withers, the world languishes and withers, the exalted of the earth languish. The earth is defiled by its people; they have disobeyed the laws, violated the statutes and broken the everlasting covenant. Therefore a curse consumes the earth; its people must bear their guilt. Therefore earth's inhabitants are burned up, and very few are left.

Other references to international judgment include Ezekiel 25 to 30; 32; 35; 38 to 39; Amos 1:3 to 2:5; the entire books of Obadiah and Jonah; and Zephaniah 2:4–15.

THE NEW COVENANT

Among the most significant prophecies revealing God's mission to the Gentiles are those about the new covenant and the future outpouring of God's Spirit.

> " 'The time is coming,' declares the LORD, 'when I will make a new covenant with the house of Israel and with the house of Judah. It will not be like the covenant I made with their forefathers when I took them by the hand to lead them out of Egypt, because they broke my covenant, though I was a husband to them,' declares the LORD. 'This is the covenant I will make with the house of Israel after that time,' declares the LORD. 'I will put my law in their minds and write it on their hearts. I will be their God, and they will be my people' " (Jer. 31:31–33).

The new covenant, though given in the context of Israel and Judah, will in fact be the basis for the Gentiles' entrance into salvation seen elsewhere by the prophets.

GOD'S MISSION OF BLESSING AS SEEN IN THE PROPHETS

The prophets also contain remarkable prophecies of restoration, including a future day in which the nations will be among the redeemed. There are numerous specific references to Gentile inclusion in the new covenant. Consider the following:

> So that from the rising of the sun to the place of its setting men may know there is none besides me. I am the Lord, and there is no other (Isa. 45:6).
>
> "Turn to me and be saved, all you ends of the earth; for I am God, and there is no other" (Isa. 45:22).
>
> "It is too small a thing for you to be my servant to restore the tribes of Jacob and bring back those of Israel I have kept. I will also make you a light for the Gentiles, that you may bring my salvation to the ends of the earth" (Isa. 49:6).
>
> "The law will go out from me; my justice will become a light to the nations. . . . My salvation is on the way, and my arm will bring justice to the nations" (Isa. 51:4–5).
>
> The Lord will lay bare his holy arm in the sight of all the nations, and all the ends of the earth will see the salvation of our God (Isa. 52:10).
>
> "These I will bring to my holy mountain and give them joy in my house of prayer. Their burnt offerings and sacrifices will be accepted on my altar; for my house will be called a house of prayer for all nations" (Isa. 56:7).
>
> "In that day I will restore David's fallen tent. I will repair its broken places, restore its ruins, and build it as it used to be, so that they may possess the remnant of Edom and all the nations that bear my name," declares the Lord, who will do these things (Amos 9:11–12).
>
> The Lord will be awesome to them when he destroys all the gods of the land. The nations on every shore will worship him, every one in its own land (Zeph. 2:11).
>
> "Shout and be glad, O Daughter of Zion. For I am coming, and I will live among you," declares the Lord. "Many nations will be joined with the Lord in that day and will become my people. I will live among you and you will know that the Lord Almighty has sent me to you. The Lord will inherit Judah as his portion in the holy land and will again choose Jerusalem. Be still before the Lord, all mankind, because he has roused himself from his holy dwelling" (Zech. 2:10–13).

The prophecy of Amos 9:11–12 is especially significant because of its prominence at the Jerusalem council; James, the Lord's brother, uses it in connection with the inclusion of Gentiles among God's people after the restoration of David's throne. James sees Jesus' resurrection as a public declaration of the renewed kingdom and the correct time to welcome Gentiles into the community of faith (Acts 15:15–19). It is especially significant that the Jerusalem council did not settle a doctrinal dispute on the basis of testimony, not even the united testimony of Peter and Paul. Rather, James appealed to Amos 9:11–12 to settle it, not as a proof text but as a text representative of a wide body of relevant Old Testament texts.

GOD'S SERVANT

In the four servant songs of Isaiah, the focus moves between the nation as servant and the future Messiah as servant. In both cases, one focus of the ministry of the servant is to be to the nations (42:6; 49:6; 51:4).[8] That Christ ideally fulfilled the Messiah's servant role is well illustrated in the Gospels and cogently summarized in Philippians 2:5–11.

THE HOLY SPIRIT TO BE OUTPOURED ON ALL PEOPLE

The prophet Joel saw the outpouring of the Spirit as being for all people, sons and daughters, old and young, resulting in the salvation of all who call upon the Lord: "'And afterward, I will pour out my Spirit on all people. Your sons and daughters will prophesy, your old men will dream dreams, your young men will see visions. Even on my servants, both men and women, I will pour out my Spirit in those days. . . . And everyone who calls on the name of the Lord will be saved; for on Mount Zion and in Jerusalem there will

---

[8]Kaiser, *Old Testament Theology*, 216.

be deliverance, as the Lord has said, among the survivors whom the Lord calls'" (Joel 2:28–29,32).

This prophecy of Joel is significant for its connection to the overall promise plan of the Old Testament. Richard D. Patterson summarizes this connection as follows:

> It must also be noted that the outpouring of the Spirit is an accompanying feature of that underlying basic divine promise given to Abraham and the patriarchs, ratified through David, reaffirmed in the terms of the new covenant, and guaranteed in the person and work of Jesus the Messiah (cf. Gen. 12:1–3; 15; 17; 2 Sam. 7:11–29; Ps. 89:3–4, 27–29 [4–5, 28–30 MT]; Jer. 31:31–34; Acts 2:29–36; 26:6–7; Gal. 3:5–14; Eph. 1:10–14; Heb. 6:13–20; 9:15).
>
> At Pentecost, then, two tributary streams of prophecy met and blended together: Christ's prophetic promise was directly fulfilled; Joel's prophecy was fulfilled but not consummated. It awaits its ultimate fulfillment but was provisionally applicable to Pentecost and the ages of the Spirit as the initial step in those last days that will culminate in the prophesied miraculous signs heralding the Day of the Lord and the events distinctive to the nation of Israel.[9]

The "'all people'" of Joel 2:28 is often viewed as meaning "all Israel" because of the words "'your sons and your daughters'" that immediately follow.[10] While these words must be considered in the interpretation of this passage, they are by no means the whole story. The intent of the passage is to expand, not delimit, the Spirit's presence. Instead of the Spirit coming on selected individuals for specific acts, the Spirit would now be poured out upon all classes and groups. In subsequent fact, the fulfillment did indeed begin with the sons and daughters of Israel, but it quickly grew toward a wider

---

[9]Richard D. Patterson, "Joel," in *The Expositor's Bible Commentary*, ed. Frank E. Gaebelein (Grand Rapids: Zondervan Publishing House, 1985), 7:258.

[10]David Allan Hubbard, *Joel and Amos*, vol. 22b of *Tyndale Old Testament Commentaries*, ed. D. J. Wiseman (Downers Grove, Ill.: InterVarsity Press, 1989), 69.

public. The future age of the Spirit would move toward all peoples, not away from them.

A somewhat parallel concept may be found in the " 'new covenant' " of Jeremiah 31:31. There, the new covenant was said to be for the house of Israel. But the prophetic stream had already swept Jeremiah into a calling as a " 'prophet to the nations' " (1:5). In point of fact, the new covenant was subsequently shown to be the means for full Gentile participation as the people of God. So, in this passage (Joel 2:28–29), while the prophetic focus may initially have been on Israel's sons and daughters, ultimately it extended to the world.

As Patterson suggested above, the significance of this revelation is that it shows a future age of the Spirit to be in God's plan of blessing the nations through the promised seed of Abraham (Gen. 12:3 et al.). This outpouring of the Holy Spirit, Joel said, would be without respect to ethnicity (if " 'all people' " is allowed to mean more than "all Israel"), gender, societal level, or age (vv. 28–29) and would result in the salvation of everyone who would call upon the name of the Lord (v. 32). Since Israel had long known that it was to mediate God's blessing to the nations, the provision that all who called upon the name of the Lord would be saved must have suggested inclusion of the Gentiles: Such a great day as Joel prophesied would certainly attract their attention—and those who called upon the Lord would be saved. All that waited was an announcement that this great day had dawned. The stage was thus set for Peter who served as God's chosen spokesman for this announcement on the Day of Pentecost (Acts 2).

These words do a great deal to "demarginalize" modern-day Pentecostalism. Joel identified the New Testament Pentecostal outpouring and subsequent ingathering from among all nations as the mainstream of the prophetic river. While every revival movement is subject to human weakness and may stand in need of correction, the extent to which modern Pentecostalism is the continuation of the Acts fulfillment of Joel's words is the extent to which it is at the center of *missio Dei*.

JONAH

The book of Jonah holds a unique place in the Old Testament development of *missio Dei*, both for God's requirement of a prophet to a Gentile people and for that people's subsequent response to His message.

While the mission of God had long been known (Jonah ministered in the eighth century B.C., well over a thousand years after Abraham), several factors are significant. First, he was sent on a redemptive mission to a Gentile city, Nineveh. Rather than his being allowed some vague notion of how Israel was to bless the nations or of blessing being centripetal (coming toward Jerusalem), Jonah was ordered to reach Nineveh. Second, the kingdom of God's universal nature is shown in several ways: Jonah cannot escape God's dominion by running away. The very truth of Jonah's message negated his fleeing from it. Next, the experiences onboard ship demonstrated God's power over nature, over Gentile sailors, and over Jewish reluctance to bless the nations. Finally, Jonah's problem was clearly demonstrated as a failure to act upon knowledge, rather than a failure to have that knowledge. From his prayer in the belly of the fish, Jonah shows he knew both the futility of idol worship by the Gentiles as well as the possibility of grace to the Gentiles (Jon. 2:8).

The city of Nineveh is shown to be under God's rule in several ways. Jonah was sent there, indicating that the city was held morally accountable by the Sovereign God. God accepted their repentance and judgment was averted. Even the animals are mentioned as objects of God's concern (4:11).

The story of the vine in chapter 4 demonstrates the extent of God's concern for Nineveh. When Jonah exhibited more compassion for the withered vine than for the people of Nineveh, God asked him if he had a right to be angry (v. 9). Jonah replied that he had a right to be angry enough to die. However, he had no claim to the land the vine grew on. He had not purchased the seed, planted the seed, cultivated the land, nor defended the land. Yet, because the plant pleased him, he felt angry over its dying to the point of dying himself. God, by contrast, had invested heavily in the Ninevites whom Jonah despised. God had created them in His own image, brought them rain and sunshine for their crops, placed the concept of eternity in their hearts, had not left himself without a witness to them, and He had just gone to a great deal of trouble to send them a reluctant prophet. In fact, God had invested more in Nineveh's cattle than Jonah had in the vine (4:11). Thus, the love of God for Gentile peoples outside the covenant is strongly stated in this book. No wonder Jesus appealed to Jonah as the sign for His sufferings and subsequent resurrection (Matt. 12:39–41).

Summary

Since God commissioned His prophets to remind the people of their covenant obligations, the prophets not only repeated those obligations but enlarged upon them. Their message contains a strong affirmation of the same *missio Dei* developed earlier in Scripture.

Indeed, the uniform testimony throughout the Old Testament of God's plan to redeem the Gentiles is a strong testimonial to the unity of the Old Testament and the inspiration of Scripture.

STUDY QUESTIONS

1. Compare Psalm 2:7 with Acts 13:33. Why is it said that the Resurrection was equivalent to an inauguration? How does this Psalm provide a theological foundation for New Testament missions?

2. Explain the key thought of Psalm 46:10, " 'Be still, and know that I am God; I will be exalted among the nations, I will be exalted in the earth.' "

3. Describe the key missiological thoughts of Psalms 47; 67; and 87. Locate at least five psalms not treated in the text that express corresponding thoughts.

4. Explain the missiological significance of Psalm 100:1.

5. What is the theological surprise of Psalm 117? How is this surprising element consistent with the *missio Dei* of the historical books? How is it foundational to New Testament revelation concerning the place of the nations in God's kingdom?

6. Describe the day the Lord has made (Ps. 118:24) within its context. How does this Psalm anticipate New Testament missions?

7. Within Proverbs and other poetic literature, how does "the fear of the Lord" function as a theme with missiological implications?

8. Describe the significance of the concept of a covenant lawsuit within the message of the prophets. How had Israel's failure to keep the covenant adversely affected the nations? Give evidence that the nations, though not under God's covenant with Israel, were nonetheless morally accountable to God.

9. Explain the missiological significance of Isaiah's servant passages, Jeremiah's prophecy of a new covenant, Joel's prophecy of the outpouring of the Spirit on all flesh, and the experiences of Jonah.

10. The prophets are replete with references to the blessing of God upon all nations. Explain this

diachronically. How had God's previous revelation prepared the way for such prophetic vision?

Chapter 3:
Missio Dei in the Gospels: Proclamation of a King

In the Gospels, we glimpse the King himself modeling the character of His reign by living among His subjects on earth. The *missio Dei* motif developed in the Old Testament is now personified in the Messiah, Jesus, explained by His teaching, and further prophesied, in both direct statement and oblique parable.

Royal Passages

From the Old Testament, we learned that the mission of God was defined by the eternal kingdom promised to David (2 Sam. 7:16; 1 Chron. 17:12–14; Ps. 89:36–37). Further, a promised seed of Abraham was to bless all nations (Gen. 12:3; 18:18; 22:18; see also 26:4 and 28:14).

Therefore, it is highly significant that Matthew opens his Gospel with the statement, "A record of the genealogy of Jesus Christ the son of David, the son of Abraham" (1:1). With this brief statement, Matthew invokes the memory of the eternal kingdom promised to David through which will be fulfilled the blessing of the nations promised to Abraham.

The rest of Matthew, and indeed the rest of the Gospels, builds upon this dual anticipation. First, the long-awaited kingdom has come in the person of Jesus Christ, the Son of David. Second, the long-awaited blessing of the nations is about to be realized through the authority and power of Jesus the Davidic King.

Understanding this is the key to reading the Gospels as disclosures of the mission of God. Without "advance organizers" in the text such as Matthew 1:1, we would be left to our own devices in arranging what might appear to be something of a random accumulation of Jesus' sayings and deeds.

Parables

A major function of the parables is to throw light upon this twin theme of kingdom and nations. Indeed, the usual introductory phrase of a parable is " 'The kingdom of heaven is like' " (Matt. 13:24). The parable then typically moves toward some expression of harvest or expansion. So what is the kingdom like? Let us look at a few examples.

It is like a farmer who sowed seed in several kinds of soil (Matt. 13:1–15,18–23; Mark 4:3–20; Luke 8:4–15). Jesus' interpretation of this parable begins with the statement, " 'The farmer sows the word' " (Mark 4:14). This statement connects the Testaments: Throughout the Old Testament period God had been known by His word. All who came into contact with the Lord in the Old Testament, whether Israelite or non-Israelite, did so through His word. The Old Testament narratives, law, wisdom literature, and prophetic discourse are all referred to in the New Testament as Scripture, or God's Word (2 Tim. 3:16). As I have tried to show, that word had as its purpose statement the words spoken to Abraham: " 'All peoples on earth will be blessed through you' " (Gen. 12:3). The organizing principle of the Old Testament is the promise of a Seed through whom will come the eternal kingdom of God and the blessing of the nations.[1]

The unceasing activity of the sower results in a thorough distribution of the seed upon all types of

---

[1]Walter C. Kaiser, *Toward an Old Testament Theology* (Grand Rapids: Zondervan Publishing House, 1978), 39.

soil.[2] So when this message of Christ and the plan He represents is made known to humanity, the responses vary according to the types of soil mentioned in the parable. This parable is central to Jesus' teaching and hence to understanding the kingdom of God. It is placed at the beginning of three major parables in all three Synoptic Gospels. And Jesus asks: " 'Don't you understand this parable? How then will you understand any parable?' " (Mark 4:13).[3]

Two conclusions may be reached about the Parable of the Sower. First, harvest is central to the teaching of Jesus and to the kingdom of God. Far from being an accidental metaphor suggested by a rural environment, harvest is rather the heart of the nature of God. In the light of the entire teaching of the Old Testament, this harvest must include the spread of the gospel to all nations. The sowing of the seed represents a divine initiative breaking in upon the soil. The seed will be sown so that all may have the opportunity to be blessed regardless of their condition of receptivity. Second, the Word of God will always divide humanity into differing groups depending upon their reception of the message. It was so in Jesus' day, and it has remained so.

With this parable serving as a key, the parable of the weeds may be unlocked (Matt. 13:24–30,36–43). In stating that " 'the field is the world' " (Matt. 13:38), Jesus is once again laying claim to all He created. False teaching is the result of illegal trespassers, and He will eventually gather its weeds and burn them, leaving His universal rule unchallenged. In this way, the ancient promise of a seed to bless all nations is finally and fully realized.

Or, the kingdom of heaven is known through the

[2]Walter W. Wessel, "Mark," in *The Expositor's Bible Commentary*, ed. Frank E. Gaebelein (Grand Rapids: Zondervan Publishing House, 1981), 9:648.

[3]R. Alan Cole, *Mark*, vol. 2 of *Tyndale New Testament Commentaries*, ed. Leon Morris (Grand Rapids: Wm. B. Eerdmans, 1989), 149–50.

parable of the eleventh-hour laborers (Matt. 19:30 to
20:16). This parable is bracketed by the statement,
" 'The last will be first, and the first will be last' " (20:16;
cf. 19:30). With the other parables already interpreted
by Christ, the landowner is quickly seen to be Christ
himself. He is the hero of the parable, diligently returning time and again throughout the day to call workers
who will labor on the basis of trusting Him. After the
entry of yet one more group of workers, who sadly had
been idle all the day, the day finishes with a one-hour
grand finale of work.

It is the Master's question to this last group of workers that links the parable to Matthew 1:1 and *missio Dei:*
" ' "Why have you been standing here all day long
doing nothing?" ' " (20:6). Jesus Christ is indeed the son
of both David and Abraham, and the time to extend
His royal rule throughout all the nations has come. In
such an atmosphere, failing to work for lack of a formal
labor contract is petty, even unthinkable, thus the question, "Why?" Even more appalling is the attitude of the
earlier laborers who ignore the glorious unfolding of
missio Dei, choosing instead to regard the progress of
divine grace throughout the world to be little more
than a social experience and a meal ticket. Their attitude naturally gives rise to jealousy over the inclusion
of "nonunion" workers when those workers are gener-
ously paid.

Several features of this parable should be noted. The
first-hour workers are the only ones with a formal contract, the standard denarius per day. The return of the
owner for more workers throughout the day is noteworthy and is consistent with his preoccupation with
harvest and with the request for the disciples to pray
for more laborers (Matt. 9:38). When Jesus promised to
pay the later workers what was " 'right' " (Gk. *dikaion,*
20:4), He may have been suggesting His own righteousness.

That the last hour was the most successful seems

required by several factors at the conclusion of the story. First, the payment of a denarius for only one hour of work shows a change of the owner's demeanor. From the time the first workers were sent out until this point, the owner had refused to waste time discussing such mundane matters as finance. His whole preoccupation was on harvest with the understanding that his righteousness guaranteed fair treatment, and therefore there was neither time nor energy to be spent going over contracts. Now with harvest over, for the first time he relaxes and shows his pleasure by the generous payment of the later workers. The pleasure may have been brought about by the quantity they were able to harvest, by their ability to harvest where others had not succeeded, or perhaps by their sacrificial service in bringing about closure to the harvest process. In any case, the generous payment is deliberately highlighted by their being paid first.

When objections come from the earlier workers, Jesus uses a word for friend (Gk. *hetaire,* v. 13) used only here, of the guest without a wedding garment (Matt. 22:12), and of Judas Iscariot (Matt. 26:50). Like the older brother in another parable (Luke 15:11–32), they refused to join in the general rejoicing of that occasion, choosing rather to sulk in their supposed mistreatment. They were not really mistreated though, since they were paid all they had been promised. Rather, they simply identified themselves as being interested in their own welfare or in maintaining the status quo rather than in the interests of the owner or his harvest. In asking, "'Are you envious because I am generous?'" (Matt. 20:15), the words of the owner are, literally, "I . . . I am" (Gk. *ego eimi*). This is the same construction used by Jesus in His seven "I am" statements in John, where they were understood to imply a claim to divinity. The same may be the case here. At the very least, they provide emphasis, that is, *I myself* am "good" (v. 15, KJV; Gk. *agathos*), probably spoken in contrast to the meanness of spirit with which the earlier workers were complaining.

The immediate setting of this parable gives keys to what it meant to those who first heard it. Children, though in many ways socially last, had just been made to be first (19:13–15). Then, the rich young man, though socially first, had just gone away last (19:16–30). Peter and the rest of the disciples had been shocked at Jesus' insistence that it is hard for the rich (the first) to enter heaven (19:24–25). Jesus had then promised a special place, when the Son of man sits on His glorious throne, for the twelve who had followed Him and for all others who similarly will forsake all and follow Him (19:28). So, these twelve would have identified themselves with the " 'last' " of Jesus' parable (20:16). They may also have seen their role in following Jesus as insignificant in comparison with that of those earlier in the day—patriarchs like Abraham, Isaac, and Jacob, or King David, or one of the prophets. After all, they had brought no kingdom but just followed Jesus, without having any place to lay their head.

Moving to present application, the "last—first" principle that brackets the parable provides its main meaning and has application for all times. Historically, missions were long thought to be primarily the preserve of the propertied and politically powerful Western nations. More recently, the fast-growing churches of the Two-Thirds World have sent missionaries until they now form a majority of those presently serving. Some churches, however, have not yet entered meaningfully into missions, due to financial constraint or other reasons. Jesus' parable speaks to such churches, and to all who feel unable to go. Those who hear His voice and go will find an atmosphere of unbelievable success, despite persecutions, as they complete the eleventh-hour harvest. They will also find unbelievable reward when the harvest has been completed.

Other Gentile References

Aside from the parables, the dual theme of David's kingdom and the blessing of the nations is suggested by Gentile passages throughout the Gospels.

When the newborn Christ was presented in the temple, Simeon declared: " 'For my eyes have seen your salvation, which you have prepared in the sight of all people, a light for revelation to the Gentiles and for glory to your people Israel' " (Luke 2:30–32).

Simeon would have known the phrase " 'light to the Gentiles' " from both Isaiah 42:6 and 49:6. The " 'all people' " are composed of both Gentiles and Israelites, the glory shining as a light from Israel to the nations as had been prophesied for centuries.

It was wise men "from the east" who came to worship (Matt. 2:1; cf. 2:2–12), anticipating the day that many would come " 'from the east and the west' " (Matt. 8:11).

It was a Gentile centurion whose faith was greater than that found in Israel (Matt. 8:10; Luke 7:9). This prompted Jesus to announce that the Kingdom would include Gentiles from around the world (Matt. 8:11). It was "a Canaanite woman" whose answer so touched Jesus that he referred to her great faith (Matt.15:22; cf. v. 28). In one of Jesus' most famous parables, the unlikely hero was a Samaritan (Luke 10:25–37).

While the commission of Matthew 10 was for a Jewish mission in the immediate future, much of the chapter deals with the Gentile mission soon to follow. As an example of this, Jesus said the disciples should expect serious persecution that would result in testifying before governors, kings, and Gentiles (Matt. 10:17–18). But there is no evidence that this happened during the mission that immediately followed. Rather, this instruction looked beyond the immediate mission to Israel, toward the impending Gentile mission.

In denouncing Jewish cities that had not repented, Jesus stated that the judgment would be more bearable for the Gentile cities of Tyre, Sidon, and even Sodom than for them (Matt. 11:21–24).

Of the Gospel references to Isaiah 56:7, Mark alone quotes the end of the verse so as not to miss its Gentile focus: "And as he taught them, he said, 'Is it not written: "My house will be called a house of prayer for all nations"? But you have made it "a den of robbers"'" (Mark 11:17; see also Matt. 21:12–13; Luke 19:45–46; John 2:13–17). These words are quoted in the context of Jesus' cleansing of the court of the Gentiles at the Jewish temple. It was this area, reserved for Gentile worship, that had been preempted for commercial purposes. Jesus' anger indicated displeasure against so blatant an affront to His intention that all nations should be blessed.

The vocabulary of the Gospel of John includes terms that anticipated a mission beyond Israel. The term "world" (Gk. *kosmos*) refers primarily to the inhabited earth and appears thirty-six times in twenty-seven verses within John. Other Greek words add a further forty-two occurrences of the English word "world." Many of these references are missiologically significant. For example, John 1:9 states, "The true light that gives light to every man was coming into the world" (Gk. *kosmos*). The two great points theologically in this verse are that Jesus was entering the world and that this entry was of significance to all people everywhere. John 1:10 adds to the weight of John 1:9 by stating that Jesus made the world: Though He would live in Israel, His redemptive mission was for the entire *kosmos*. In John 3:16–17, the word *kosmos* is used three times in describing the mission of the Son, sent by God to bring eternal life rather than "'to condemn the world'" (v. 17; Gk. *kosmos*). The phrase "'all men'" is used in a sense that would imply Gentiles in John 1:7 and 12:32. The term "whoever" is used six times in John's Gospel in the traditional sense of persons of any origin.

Also within John, it was to a Samaritan woman that

Jesus gave a clear statement of messiahship (John 4:26). Jesus used this occasion to explain to His disciples, " 'My food . . . is to do the will of him who sent me and to finish his work' " (John 4:34), for the fields were already " 'ripe for harvest' " (John 4:35). On this same occasion, the Samaritans—recognizing that they, too, were included in the kingdom of God—exclaimed, " 'We know that this man really is the Savior of the world' " (v. 42; Gk. *kosmos*). Indeed, Jesus had " 'other sheep' " that would be included: " 'There shall be one flock and one shepherd' " (John 10:16). " 'All men,' " Jesus prophesied, would be drawn to Him when He was " 'lifted up' " (i.e., on a cross, John 12:32).

In an unusual reference, the High Priest Caiaphas's prophecy of Jesus' death is interpreted by John to be for all peoples who, in turn, are made one: "Then one of them, named Caiaphas, who was high priest that year, spoke up, 'You know nothing at all! You do not realize that it is better for you that one man die for the people than that the whole nation perish.' He did not say this on his own, but as high priest that year he prophesied that Jesus would die for the Jewish nation, and not only for that nation but also for the scattered children of God, to bring them together and make them one" (John 11:49–52).

When Greeks attending a feast at Jerusalem requested an audience with Jesus, Jesus used the occasion to say that a kernel of wheat must die in order to produce " 'many seeds' " (John 12:24). In this way, He was anticipating the benefit to the Gentiles resulting from His own death (John 12:20–26).

Significantly, John viewed the accomplishment of Christ's anticipated harvest as being accomplished through the convicting power of the Holy Spirit: " 'When he comes, he will convict the world of guilt in regard to sin and righteousness and judgment: in regard to sin, because men do not believe in me; in regard to righteousness, because I am going to the

Father, where you can see me no longer; and in regard to judgment, because the prince of this world now stands condemned'" (John 16:8–11).

Commission

The Great Commission passages that end each Gospel are the logical conclusion to the twin motifs of kingdom and nations (Matt. 28:18–20; Mark 16:15–18; Luke 24:46–49 together with Acts 1:8; John 20:21). As Isaiah had prophesied, the restoration of the Davidic kingdom was to usher in a day in which the Kingdom would be extended to Gentiles. The "Jewish only" era of the Kingdom would be unable to contain the glory of that greater day (Isa. 49:6).

The commission passages agree with the kingdom/nations motif in the following ways: First, the commission is given upon the basis of Christ's authority (Gk. *exousia*), a kingdom reference. It is the resurrected Christ who has full royal authority and thus moves quickly to include all His realm—the " 'all nations'" of Matthew 28:19. All the subjects of Christ's kingdom must receive the royal announcement of the gospel (Mark 16:15); the word "'preach'" in Mark 16:15 may be used of the proclamation of a king (cf. NEB, "proclaim"). Further, "'all nations'" are to be discipled and taught to observe all kingdom regulations, "'everything I have commanded you'" (Matt. 28:19–20; cf. Matt. 5 to 7). Baptism in the name of the Father, Son, and Holy Spirit (Matt. 28:19) implies both the mission of the triune God and an understanding of that mission on the part of those being baptized. All those who proceed to the nations as the King's ambassadors are first to receive a mighty empowerment of the King's own Spirit (Luke 24:49; Acts 1:8).

Perhaps John records the most comprehensive kingdom meaning of the commission: " 'As the Father has sent me, I am sending you'" (John 20:21). The Father had sent Jesus as the divine Son of David to bring

God's kingdom to earth. In this statement of transferred apostleship, Jesus squarely places His kingdom
mission upon the shoulders of His apostles. As Jesus
finished His mission of dying for the sins of the world,
so the Church is commissioned to finish its mission of
making disciples of all nations. As Jesus moved in the
power of the Holy Spirit, so the disciples are to move in
the power of the same Holy Spirit. As Jesus represented
His Father's will with acts of compassion and attention
to the oppressed, so must the Church be characterized
by such acts. As Jesus prepared the Church for worldwide witness through eschatological statements, so the
Church must use these prophetic discourses to mobi-
lize itself to fulfill Christ's witness throughout the
earth. As Jesus bypassed the power structures of His
day by calling and empowering simple fishermen to be
apostles, so the Church must retain a simple trust in
God's power among ordinary people to accomplish
everything God has willed.

If Christ's commission did not extend to all the
nations of the Gentiles, then He would be more of a
tribal chieftain than a king. It is the very essence of
God's kingdom that it must be worldwide. Satan's
quest to be like God has led to his continual attempt to
gain recognition of his own kingdom; this was apparently one of his objectives in tempting Jesus. Bringing
people from all nations to serve Christ deprives Satan's
counterfeit kingdom of even the pretense of legitimacy.
Any subtraction from believers among all peoples is
thus the reduction of the essential nature of Christ's
kingdom to the level of a counterfeit. For the Kingdom
to be the Kingdom it must be composed of all nations.
When the risen Jesus stated that all authority was given
to Him, He was announcing to His followers that the
time had come to claim all people groups as His legiti-
mate kingdom inheritance (Matt. 28:18; cf. Ps. 2:8).

One further note: It has already been pointed out that
John's Great Commission is in 20:21, " 'As the Father

has sent me, I am sending you.'" This verse should be read as a sequel to 17:4: "'I have brought you glory on earth by completing the work you gave me to do.'" Since the Church is sent as Jesus was, and Jesus completed His assignment by going all the way to the cross, so the Church must finish its assigned task of preaching the gospel to all the world. How could it be otherwise?

Teaching

The ethical and moral teachings of Jesus should likewise be seen in the context of His kingdom. These teachings invite the hungry of the nations, the weary and heavy laden, to come to Jesus' kingdom and find rest, protection, and purpose. The endless cycles of dehumanizing fear and the manipulation of spirits common to the Gentiles stand in stark contrast to the simple life of faith and honesty taught by Christ. The teachings of Christ represent the fulfillment of the Old Testament law and the perfection of Old Testament wisdom. If the Old Testament covenant community had a much better life than their neighbors, how much greater the difference is now between those whose lives truly reflect Christ's kingdom and those whose lives tragically miss the mark. This difference serves as the validation of the gospel proclaimed by the Church.

Prophecy

The prophetic portions are likewise given as prior statements of the future scope and power of the Kingdom. Since the King will rule all nations, those in rebellion should quickly surrender to the divine King and be included as loyal subjects. Otherwise, they will be weeded out of His kingdom (Matt.13:41).

It should be noted that Jesus makes a strong correlation between the successful completion of His mission to all nations and the coming of the end. Matthew 24:14

reads, " 'And this gospel of the kingdom will be preached in the whole world as a testimony to all nations, and then the end will come.' " Mark 13:10 conveys the same thought: " 'And the gospel must first be preached to all nations.' "

A helpful note on Matthew 24:14 appears in the *Full Life Study Bible:* "Only God will know when this task is accomplished according to his purpose. The believer's task is to faithfully and continually press on 'to all nations' till the Lord returns to take his church to heaven. . . . We must live in a tension between the imminency of Christ's coming and the fact that Christ has commanded us to keep on spreading the gospel."[4]

Unreached people groups indicate something incomplete rather than " 'the end' " (Gk. *telos,* "consummation") that the Kingdom is headed for. The Church should address these gaps in completing the Kingdom so imperfection might be removed and the Kingdom's destiny be completed. The Church has no choice but to continue to associate, as Jesus did, the geographical and ethnic expansion of the preaching of the gospel with the completion of its task (Matt. 24:14).

Those who have a holy longing for the realization of Christ's kingdom are motivated to honor their king by extending His present rule to the most remote or most resistant portions of the earth. Prophecy as given by Jesus serves as the announcement that the mission will be successfully completed. It motivates His followers to offer themselves willingly in His service to accomplish His mission. In Jesus' worldview, missions and eschatology were closely related.

---

[4]Donald C. Stamps, ed., *The Full Life Study Bible* (Grand Rapids: Zondervan Publishing House, 1992), 1454.

STUDY QUESTIONS

1. Explain from antecedent Scripture why Matthew 1:1 is viewed as an "advance organizer" to the remainder of the New Testament.

2. Why is the Parable of the Sower regarded as the key to understanding all Jesus' parables? How does this understanding of this parable connect to the antecedent Scriptures of the Old Testament? What does it say concerning the mission of God in the New Testament era?

3. What message does Jesus' parable of the eleventh-hour workers convey to those in our time who feel they may have been left out of participating in earth's harvest drama?

4. Demonstrate from both the Synoptic Gospels and John's Gospel that Christ viewed His mission as one to all nations.

5. Explain the Great Commission texts, which each Gospel closes with, in terms of their relationship to God's ongoing mission within history.

6. Explain the statement, "In Jesus' worldview, missions and eschatology were closely related."

Chapter 4:

Missio Dei in Acts and the Pauline Epistles: the Church in Action

Acts and the Epistles record the initial fulfillment of Christ's prophecy, " 'I will build my church' " (Matt. 16:18). They show what He continued to do through the believers by the power of the Holy Spirit. In the midst of difficulties and opposition, the Church was triumphant.

Witnesses

With Jesus' statement to the apostles that they were to be His witnesses, He established the foundation for the expansion of the gospel. It would touch Jerusalem, Judea, and Samaria on its way " 'to the ends of the earth' " (Acts 1:8). The mission, therefore, is the same *missio Dei* I have been tracing.

With the crucifixion and resurrection of Christ, the time had come for the gospel to spread rapidly, and that is exactly what it did. The apostles' role was simply that of witnesses, and they could do nothing less than tell what they had seen and heard (Acts 4:33; 1 John 1:1–3).

Note their commission and responsibility: It was God who acted first, sending Jesus into the world and raising Him from the dead, thereby proclaiming the universal dimensions of His kingdom. Then it was God the Holy Spirit directing the drama of worldwide witness. For their part, the apostles were to move obediently among the nations of the world as witnesses to all peoples. In every case, the emphasis is upon the mission of God accomplished by servants obedient to the heavenly vision—that is, under God's direction (Acts 26:19).

Gentile Tongues

An effusion of Gentile tongues—signaling the worldwide expansion of the gospel witness that was to follow—marked the initial outpouring of the Holy Spirit upon the apostles.[1] Significantly, speaking in tongues by Gentiles occurs throughout Acts as successive people groups hear the message, believe it, and are incorporated into the Church (Acts 8:14–19[by inference]; 10:46; and 19:6).

Each people group reached with the gospel is thus designated as full participants in the mission of getting the gospel to the remainder of the peoples of the world.

Don Richardson analyzes the significance of the miracle of Pentecost as follows:

> But wait—regarding that bestowal of the Holy Spirit's power—suppose God had hired you as a public relations expert to plan the event for Him! Suppose He had given you just one specification—it must happen in a manner which will make absolutely clear to even the dullest disciple that the power about to be bestowed is not merely for the personal blessing or exaltation of the recipients, but rather to enable them to take the gospel across the world to all peoples.
>
> Even if you were the most ingenious public relations consultant of all time, you probably would not have fantasized a clearer way to get that point across than the following. . . .
>
> The power of the Holy Spirit coming upon the apostles and other faithful followers of Jesus caused them to speak miraculously in the many Gentile languages represented by the throng of diaspora Jews and Gentile converts then gathered in Jerusalem. Why? . . .
>
> Seen in the context of Jesus' ministry and His clearly

---

[1]Don Richardson, *Eternity In Their Hearts* (Ventura, Calif.: Regal Books, 1981), 156–57.

articulated plans for the whole world, the bestowal of that miraculous outburst of *Gentile* languages could have only one main purpose: to make crystal clear that the Holy Spirit's power was and is bestowed with the specific goal of the evangelization of all peoples in view![2]

The Book of Acts records what seems to be a reluctant advance of the New Testament Church across social and political borders. Though the believers shared a common Pentecostal experience, the missiological ramifications of that experience appear to have been understood only gradually.

If, as Richardson suggests, Pentecostal tongues provided a significant object lesson for the Early Church, perhaps there may be a correlation between the practice of speaking in tongues and the growth of churches among modern Pentecostals. In any case, Pentecostal churches are notable for emphasizing the Spirit's empowerment of all believers so that they may bring in the last-day harvest. Joel's prophesied Pentecostal experience has resulted in churches that win the lost in country after country around the world. Many have argued that changed lives are the best recommendation of Christianity to a watching non-Christian world. In the same way, Spirit-empowered Christian witness may be the best recommendation of Pentecostal experience to watching Christians of non-Pentecostal tradition. Those who experience today what the apostles experienced at Pentecost have taken a major step toward that empowered witness.

All People

Peter, in his Pentecost sermon,[3] cited Joel's prophecy of an outpouring of the Holy Spirit upon all people.

---

[2]Ibid., Richardson's emphasis.
[3]Actually not a sermon in the modern sense but a manifestation of the Holy Spirit's gift of prophecy: Peter spoke spontaneously as the Spirit enabled him. The same root verb is used of Peter's speaking as is used of speaking in tongues in Acts 2:4.

Though in Acts 2 it was not yet time for Peter to press it, Joel clearly prophesied the worldwide dimension that was ahead for God's kingdom.

This Pentecost event and Peter's scriptural exposition (Acts 2:14–36) background his preaching to the Gentile Cornelius and his household (Acts 10). He summarized the message of all the prophets for the assembled Gentiles as being " 'that everyone who believes in him receives forgiveness of sins through his name' " (Acts 10:43, an apparent reference to Joel 2:32); at this point God supernaturally intervened to confirm Peter's message by pouring out the Holy Spirit upon them (Acts 10:44–46). The fact that the Gentiles spoke in tongues was accepted to mean they had received the same experience as had the Jews at Pentecost (10:45–46; 11:15–17). Though this event would not solve the debate over circumcision (see Acts 15), it is a clear statement that God had accepted Gentiles into the community of faith. In so doing, God had opened the door for full Gentile participation in His mission.

In Acts 2:16, Peter had stated that the scene witnessed by the gathering crowd was what Joel had prophesied. In Acts 11:17, Peter states that Cornelius and the other Gentiles received " 'the same [Gk. *isên*, "identical"] gift' " as that received by the Jews on the Day of Pentecost. It therefore may be concluded that what was received by the household of Cornelius was also that spoken of by Joel. It may further be concluded that similar manifestations of the Holy Spirit throughout church history stand in this same tradition. Though no one like Peter is present to have witnessed both New Testament and current phenomena, the modern Pentecostal movement sees itself as the present fulfillment of what Joel prophesied. The focus is upon harvest, the laborers come from the " 'all people' " (Joel 2:28) who are receiving the promised Holy Spirit around the world, and the anticipation of judgment spoken by Joel continues to impart a sense of urgency.

All nations are now empowered as full members in Christ's witnessing and serving Church so as to fulfill every prophetic word of Scripture spoken concerning our times.

Another Prophet

After the healing of the crippled man in Acts 3, Peter cites Deuteronomy 18:15,18–19: " 'For Moses said, "The Lord your God will raise up for you a prophet like me from among your own people; you must listen to everything he tells you. Anyone who does not listen to him will be completely cut off from among his people" ' " (Acts 3:22–23).

Peter uses this passage to point out to his audience that favorable response to Jesus is not optional. The only way to remain in favor with God is to receive His long-awaited Messiah. Peter then goes on to identify " 'these days' " as the time foretold by " 'all the prophets from Samuel on' " (Acts 3:24). Finally, he quotes Genesis 22:18: " 'And you are heirs of the prophets and of the covenant God made with your fathers. He said to Abraham, "Through your offspring all peoples on earth will be blessed." When God raised up his servant, he sent him first to you to bless you by turning each of you from your wicked ways.' " (Acts 3:25–26).

Though Peter's audience is Jewish, his message contains what I. Howard Marshall refers to as a "quiet hint" of a future blessing to Gentiles.[4] Marshall goes on to state: "The little word *first* should not be overlooked. Here is the first explicit statement in Acts that historically the gospel came first to the Jews. But the promise in the previous verse suggests that the thought 'and also for the Gentiles' is implicit, and there may well be the warning that if the Jews fail to respond the

---

[4]I. Howard Marshall, *Acts*, vol. 5 of *Tyndale New Testament Commentaries*, ed. Leon Morris (Leicester, England: InterVarsity Press, 1989), 96.

Christian mission will turn to the Gentiles."[5]

When the verses are viewed as a composite, the "quiet hint" expands to suggest that the prophet like Moses will inaugurate a new day with blessing even to Gentiles, and those who oppose this will be cut off. Acts subsequently shows this to be exactly what happened.

Stephen: *Missio Dei* as a Defense

In Acts 7 Stephen's answer to his accusers is a brilliant defense of the mission of God. Though he answered the charges against him, his speech was designed more to tell the plan of God than to gain an acquittal from the charges.

The charge that Stephen had spoken blasphemy against Moses and God is given in Acts 6:11. This charge is repeated in 6:13, emending " 'Moses' " to " 'law' " and " 'God' " to " 'this holy place' " (i.e., the temple, since it was believed to be sacred as the abode of God).

Stephen's defense demonstrates from the Law that God has always been on a mission, and those who refuse to advance with Him are the true rebels. Though Stephen was killed, Paul's later theological writings concerning God, the Messiah, and the Church are all consistent with the foundations laid in Stephen's speech. Indeed, the nature of Paul's apostolate may be viewed as the logical extension of Stephen's discourse.

One of Stephen's primary concerns was to demonstrate that God's dominion included the whole earth, not just the land of Israel. Where had God first appeared to Abraham? It was in Mesopotamia, even before he traveled to Haran, neither of which was in Israel. In fact, God did not give Abraham so much as a foot of ground in Israel. Rather, He gave him a rela-

---

[5]Ibid., Marshall's emphasis.

tionship based on a promise and symbolized by the covenant mark of circumcision. Abraham's descendants were to be content with this promise for 400 years. Later, Abraham's descendant Joseph became a great man. The source of his greatness was that " 'God was with him' " (Acts 7:9), and the place where God was with him was Egypt, not Israel. So, both Abraham and Joseph demonstrate that the sovereign God manifests His presence to those fulfilling His mission in the world even though living far from Israel.

When the time drew near for the promise to be fulfilled, God appeared to Moses—not in Israel but in the land of Midian. God even declared the place where He appeared to Moses, though far from Israel, to be "holy" ground (v. 33). Then Moses " 'did wonders and miraculous signs' " for forty years—not in Israel, but in Egypt, at the Red Sea, and in the desert (v. 36). " 'This is that Moses who told the Israelites, "God will send you a prophet like me from your own people" ' " (v. 37). This was also the same Moses who was with the angel and received the law—at Sinai, not Israel.

Of course, Stephen insisted, our fathers refused to obey Moses and rejected the presence of God that was manifested in the portable tabernacle of the Testimony throughout their desert wanderings. Though Joshua brought this portable tabernacle into the Promised Land and David desired to build it a permanent house, it was Solomon who actually built the house for God. Then Stephen cited Old Testament references concerning the temple consistent with the *missio Dei* history he had just recited. Amazingly, God had declared that He did not dwell in houses made by men, for He was sovereign over all creation (vv. 48–50, citing Isa. 66:1–2; see also 1 Kings 8:27; 2 Chron. 2:6). How could people use materials made by the hand of God to restrict God's presence from actively pursuing His interests everywhere (vv. 48–50)? The true rebels were those who, like their fathers, had uncircumcised hearts and ears and had always resisted, persecuted, and killed those who truly represented the universal creator God. It is the Holy Spirit they resisted, because they insisted upon the pagan concept of a static deity. They had even killed the Righteous One, that is, the one prophesied by Moses whom they pretended to obey. While Stephen followed the mobile God, his critics attempted to redefine the sphere of God's reign until He would be little more than a tribal deity.

Though Stephen was killed, the force of his argument was recognized by his opponents, including Saul of Tarsus, and has continued to ring through the centuries. God is an active, moving God who refuses any human effort to restrict His mission. This motion is directional: moving from those in covenant to those not yet in covenant. Those who would serve Him must be friendly to this mission.

Paul: Promise as a Defense

Throughout Acts, Luke sees the expansion of the gospel to the nations as a fulfillment of promise.

The Holy Spirit is poured out upon all because " 'the promise is for you and your children and for all who are far off—for all whom the Lord our God will call' " (Acts 2:39). In days of old, God kept His promise to Abraham (Acts 7:17), and in Acts it is announced that He has now kept His promise by sending Jesus the Savior (13:23). The resurrection of Jesus from the dead is seen as a fulfillment of God's promise to David (13:32–37).

The promise, however, goes beyond the facts concerning the death and resurrection of Jesus. It also includes the proclamation of this gospel to the nations of the world. In Acts 26:6–7 Paul specifically attributes his arrest to his fervent belief in God's ability to keep this promise. Yet, from reading Acts 21:28 it is apparent that the portion of the promise most responsible for Paul's detention was God's determination (or promise) that the gospel must go to the Gentiles. In fact, the

Gentile motif is one of the most significant features in these chapters.

In Acts 21:27–29 it was Paul's fraternizing with the Gentile Trophimus that occasioned his arrest. It is noteworthy how much Paul's Jewish audience tolerated the content of his defense (Acts 22:1–21), including a detailed account of his conversion and early post-conversion experiences. They did not interrupt him even though he made references to Jesus of Nazareth (v. 8), divine healing (v. 13), Christian teaching (i.e., Paul's teaching) being identified with " ' "the God of our fathers" ' " (v. 14), Jesus as the " ' "Righteous One" ' " (v. 14), water baptism as an expression of faith in Him (v. 16), persecution to come (v. 18), and Stephen's martyrdom (v. 20). He was violently interrupted, however, when he related his specific commission to go to the Gentiles (vv. 21–22). Suggesting that God's covenant had expanded to the Gentiles was so odious to the Jewish audience that they were ready to " 'rid the earth of him!' " (v. 22). Paul had to be rescued by the Roman commander.

Thus, when Paul tells the Gentile Agrippa, " 'It is because of my hope in what God has promised our fathers that I am on trial today. . . . O king, it is because of this hope that the Jews are accusing me' " (26:6–7), it must be recognized that the portion of the promise to the fathers, specifically to Abraham (Gen. 12:3), most offensive to Paul's accusers was its inclusion of Gentiles. Paul is attributing his arrest specifically to that part of the Old Testament promise that foretold the blessing through Christ of Gentiles such as Agrippa. Paul then tells how he, too, had opposed Christian believers until his Damascus Road experience, in which Jesus specifically sent him to Gentiles so that they might be forgiven their sins and be given a place among the people of God (26:17–18). Finally, in 26:23, Paul boldly asserts that he is saying nothing beyond that taught by Moses and the prophets, " 'that the Christ would suffer and, as the first to rise from the dead, would proclaim light to his own people and to the Gentiles'" (v. 23). Paul, like Stephen before him, is thus taking the position that he is within historic Judaism and therefore not guilty under Roman law of proclaiming a new (and hence illicit) religion. Paul's "promise" defense amounts to a brilliant statement of there indeed being a single promise plan throughout history, a plan finding its fulfillment in the present unfolding of God's mission to the Gentiles.

Paul's insistence that Jesus would rise from the dead and "'proclaim light to his own people and to the Gentiles'" (Acts 26:23) so shocked Festus that he cried out saying Paul was out of his mind (v. 24). The idea of resurrection was foolishness to him. And since, as a pagan, he blindly accepted the validity of a multitude of gods, each with its national devotees, I believe Paul's insistence on a single salvation plan for all peoples must have seemed radical to him too.

Now comes the amazing part. Far from flinching at Festus' outburst, Paul appealed to Agrippa's knowledge of Scripture to support his message about Jesus' death, resurrection, and offer of salvation of all peoples. He banked on Agrippa's ability to see the truth and thus confirm that even though Paul preached to Gentiles he was still worshiping the God of his fathers as allowed by Rome and was therefore not liable to criminal prosecution.

Agrippa's subsequent response would indicate that Paul was successful in this argument (26:32).

The "Pauline Cycle"

The process used by Paul to start churches in the book of Acts has been called the "Pauline Cycle."[6] By studying church growth within Acts, one may identify

---

[6]For a detailed treatment of the "Pauline Cycle," see David Hesselgrave, *Planting Churches Cross-Culturally* (Grand Rapids: Baker Book House, 1980), 58–63.

stages of development. Typically, Paul made a deliberate attempt to start a local assembly. He and his party gathered facts, made contacts, presented the gospel, gathered and taught converts. The maturing assembly then sent its own workers out into the harvest field. The normal picture of Acts and the Epistles is of growing assemblies fulfilling their destiny by intentionally reproducing themselves.

MIRACLES

Acts begins where the Gospels left off with respect to the place of miracles within the experience of believers. Jesus had said, " 'I tell you the truth, anyone who has faith in me will do what I have been doing. He will do even greater things than these, because I am going to the Father'" (John 14:12). Acts records the growth of the Church from Jerusalem "'to the ends of the earth'" (1:8), and every chapter of that growth presupposes the Holy Spirit's presence to perform the miraculous.

Early in Acts the healing of the man born lame became the occasion for the proclamation of the gospel, with the result that "the number of men grew to about five thousand" (4:4), and the leaders of the Jews received a strong witness. Acts 5 records the manifestation of the Lord's power both in the judgment of Ananias and Sapphira and in the healing of the multitudes who brought their sick to the streets hoping simply for Peter's shadow to touch them. In Acts 8, there were great signs and miracles as Philip preached to the Samaritans. In the next chapter, Paul's conversion is marked first by a miraculous light and voice and then by his healing, as hands were laid upon him by Ananias. In the same chapter, Aeneas was healed after a paralysis of eight years and then Tabitha was raised from the dead. Peter was miraculously released from prison in chapter 12, and then Herod was fatally smitten as a judgment from God.

The rest of Acts covers Paul's ministry, a ministry consisting of Spirit-energized preaching and teaching and accompanied by miracles. The sick were healed and demons cast out; God spoke through visions and protected Paul and his party from evil men, the elements of nature, and snakebite. Acts 19:11–12 records: "God did extraordinary miracles through Paul, so that even handkerchiefs and aprons that had touched him were taken to the sick, and their illnesses were cured and the evil spirits left them."

So great was Paul's success that travelling Jewish exorcists attempted to appropriate the name of Jesus as preached by him. The record says that "all the Jews and Greeks who lived in the province of Asia heard the word of the Lord" (19:10).

MISSIONARY EPISTLES

Paul wrote his epistles to instruct churches and individuals in the theological and practical issues important to young mission churches. In other words, he wrote as a missionary would. For that reason, I call his letters missionary epistles.

Romans is a book of universals. All have sinned (3:23) and all are guilty before God (3:19). God is the God of both Jews and Gentiles (3:29). Salvation is by faith so that it may be as readily available to Gentiles as to Jews (4:16). There is one Lord for both Jew and Gentile (10:12). Paul then describes the common process by which Jew or Gentile must be saved: " 'Everyone who calls on the name of the Lord will be saved.' How, then, can they call on the one they have not believed in? And how can they believe in the one of whom they have not heard? And how can they hear without someone preaching to them? And how can they preach unless they are sent? As it is written, 'How beautiful are the feet of those who bring good news!' " (10:13–15). This process implies intentional participation by the Church in fulfilling the mission of God.

Though Paul carefully maintains his passionate love for Israel (9:1–5; 10:1), he also values his ministry as "apostle to the Gentiles" (11:13). The two are not incompatible since the Gentile ministry will itself result in the eventual salvation of Jews (11:13–14). After the full number of Gentiles has come in, all Israel will be saved (11:25–26). In view of such a majestic plan, the redeemed in Rome are to offer themselves as living sacrifices to fulfill God's mission (12:1).

The promises made to the patriarchs assure the conversion of Gentiles (15:8), their being included as people of God, a people ruled by the Root of Jesse (15:9–12).

Borrowing from Exodus 19:5–6, Paul declares his priestly duty to be the proclamation of the gospel so that the Gentiles may become acceptable to God (Rom. 15:16). In this way, those who have not seen will see (15:21; see Isa. 52:15). Such a mission is worthy of both financial support (Rom. 15:24) and prayer support (15:30). In this way, God's command that all nations hear the gospel will be fulfilled (16:26; see also 10:14–15). Romans 16:26 should be seen as a Pauline reference to the Great Commission: God's mystery is "now revealed and made known through the prophetic writings by the command of the eternal God, so that all nations might believe and obey him."

The Corinthian letters illustrate the universal applicability of the gospel as several uniquely Gentile problems are forcefully addressed. To begin with, has Christ really died for Gentiles? In 2 Corinthians 5:14–15, Paul twice states that Christ "died for all." God has given us the ministry of reconciliation (2 Cor. 5:18), since "God was reconciling the world to himself in Christ" (2 Cor. 5:19). So great is God's love for the nations that "we" are appointed ambassadors to implore the nations to be reconciled to God (2 Cor. 5:20). The Corinthians are urged not to receive God's grace in vain (2 Cor. 6:1).

They are a genuine church, able to participate in an international relief project (2 Cor. 8 and 9). Their maturity will free Paul for further service in "the regions beyond" (2 Cor. 10:16; see also Rom. 15:20).

In Galatians, the Abrahamic Scriptures from Genesis are interpreted with reference to Christ. Two points are especially significant. First, Paul states that the gospel was preached to Abraham: "The Scripture foresaw that God would justify the Gentiles by faith, and announced the gospel in advance to Abraham: 'All nations will be blessed through you'" (Gal. 3:8). Paul has earlier made a strong case that there is only one gospel (1:6–8). This brings us to the second point: Christ was the one prophesied: "The promises were spoken to Abraham and to his seed. The Scripture does not say 'and to seeds,' meaning many people, but 'and to your seed,' meaning one person, who is Christ" (Gal. 3:16). This is consistent with Jesus' words, "'Your father Abraham rejoiced at the thought of seeing my day; he saw it and was glad'" (John 8:56).

The point is that God's revelation in Genesis that all nations would be blessed through Abraham was indeed a summary statement of the gospel referring to Christ and was so understood by Abraham. In view of such an all-encompassing promise, Gentile believers are warned to remain children of that promise (Gal. 4:21–31) and not to be enticed to return to the pedagogy of Jewish legalism (4:1–7).

Ephesians argues for the unity of Christ's Church as a single body without respect to Jewish or Gentile origin. This is because both share equally in a single promise plan: "This mystery is that through the gospel the Gentiles are heirs together with Israel, members together of one body, and sharers together in the promise in Christ Jesus" (Eph. 3:6). Such a united Church will demonstrate the wisdom of God's eternal purpose (3:10–11). This picture stands behind the later description of gifts of ministry (4:11). A church that is not oriented to fulfilling God's mission has little need for any such gifts, unless they are gifts of correction.

For such believers, whether Jewish or Gentile, even persecution will advance the gospel (Phil. 1:12) as believers identify with Christ's humiliation (2:5–11) and patiently await His return from heaven (1 Thess. 1:10; 2:19; 3:13; 4:13–18; 5:23).

The servant attitude of those who would fulfill God's mission should be that of Christ, as described by Paul:

> "Your attitude should be the same as that of Christ Jesus: Who, being in very nature God, did not consider equality with God something to be grasped, but made himself nothing, taking the very nature of a servant, being made in human likeness. And being found in appearance as a man, he humbled himself and became obedient to death—even death on a cross! Therefore God exalted him to the highest place and gave him the name that is above every name, that at the name of Jesus every knee should bow, in heaven and on earth and under the earth, and every tongue confess that Jesus Christ is Lord, to the glory of God the Father" (Phil. 2:5–11).

Colossians deals with the problem of a diluted Christology, the result of the non-Christian environment in which the church was founded. As Paul mentored his younger associates, he wrote to them. First and 2 Timothy and Titus specifically deal with qualifications for the missionary vocation, how to direct the affairs of the local church, and practical concerns resulting from faulty eschatology.

IMAGE OF GOD

The Epistles refer to the Genesis concept of humanity being made in God's image. Colossians 3:10, for example, says we "have put on the new self, which is being renewed in knowledge in the image of its Creator." This would indicate that, though all are created in God's image in the sense that all are capable of coming to know God, growth in grace is likewise growth into a more perfect representation of His image. In a similar expression, Ephesians 4:22–24 speaks of putting off old behavior and putting on a "new self" (v. 24). Second Corinthians 3:18 then states: "And we, who with unveiled faces all reflect the Lord's glory, are being transformed into his likeness [image] with ever-increasing glory, which comes from the Lord, who is the Spirit."

STUDY QUESTIONS

1. What was the significance of the effusion of Gentile tongues on the Day of Pentecost? How does this phenomenon relate to Acts 1:8?

2. Relate Acts 1:8 to the following features of Acts: Stephen's defense, the "Pauline Cycle", the function of the miraculous, and Paul's "promise" defense.

3. Explain why the Pauline Epistles are called "missionary epistles." Include specific references to the nations (or Gentiles). Explain the relation of the Church and missions in Ephesians.

4. Why is Romans considered to contain an argument for missions? Summarize the arguments for universal moral accountability and the universal responsibility of believers to proclaim the gospel to all those who have not heard.

5. Explain how Galatians 3:8 and 16 interpret the promise of God to Abraham in the Book of Genesis.

Chapter 5:

Missio Dei in the General Epistles and Revelation: Mission Accomplished

The General Epistles

The General Epistles give a strong witness to *missio Dei.* Although the Book of Hebrews is directed to Jewish Christians, it is a profoundly New Testament book. The writer demonstrates the discontinuity between the old and new covenants, emphasizing the new as "better" (Heb. 7:19,22). Once the Jewish believers accept the new covenant as "better," the mission of God will lead them into all the will of God.

Though missions is not the focus of the Book of Hebrews, it is, nevertheless, fully consistent with Paul's missionary epistles (to predominantly Gentile churches): Its insistence upon a new and better divine economy finds similar arguments in Paul's epistles. As in those epistles, Hebrews lets the reader know that allegiance to the risen Christ will result in the believer being fully equipped to do His will as it pleases Him (Heb. 13:20–21)—and of course that will leads invariably to the nations.

James is an early New Testament book of practical wisdom having a theme reminiscent of both the Old Testament Wisdom Literature and of Jesus' Sermon on the Mount. A sin-weary world is attracted to such wisdom, especially when it characterizes a church where healings and miracles are the order of the day (James 5:13–18). James also includes a reference to the "image

of God" (Gen. 1:27): "With the tongue we praise our
Lord and Father, and with it we curse men, who have
been made in God's likeness" (James 3:9).

Peter assures "God's elect, strangers" (1 Pet. 1:1), that
though they were once not a people, they are now the
people of God (2:9–10). With this passage Peter builds
upon the "my people—not my people" theme of
Hosea, and here he refers primarily to Gentile believers
in strange lands who are now the covenant people of
God. His "royal priesthood" (1 Pet. 2:9) reference is
likewise an application of Exodus 19:5–6 to the present
people of God, whether Jewish or Gentile. In common
with Exodus and Paul's use of this theme (Rom. 15:16),
Peter intends his readers to see their priestly position as
a platform for praising the God who rescued them
from their former "darkness" (1 Pet. 2:9). He sees the
preaching that led to their faith as directly fulfilling Old
Testament prophecy, come to them "by the Holy Spirit
sent from heaven" (1 Pet. 1:12). In view of the nearness
of "the end of all things" (1 Pet. 4:7), Peter urges that
the various forms of spiritual gifts then common in the
local assembly be used "to serve others" (1 Pet. 4:10).

In his second epistle, Peter directly links Christ's
coming to the patience of God, prolonging the opportunity of salvation for the perishing:

> But do not forget this one thing, dear friends: With the
> Lord a day is like a thousand years, and a thousand years
> are like a day. The Lord is not slow in keeping his promise,
> as some understand slowness. He is patient with you, not
> wanting anyone to perish, but everyone to come to repen-
> tance . . . .
>
> Since everything will be destroyed in this way, what
> kind of people ought you to be? You ought to live holy and
> godly lives as you look forward to the day of God and
> speed its coming. That day will bring about the destruc-
> tion of the heavens by fire, and the elements will melt in
> the heat . . . .
>
> Bear in mind that our Lord's patience means salvation,
> just as our dear brother Paul also wrote you with the wis-
> dom that God gave him (2 Pet. 3:8–9,11–12,15).

This is no denial of Christ's imminent return. Rather, it is a statement that those who look for Christ's return should live purposefully, recognizing apparent delay as God's compassion for the lost. Some fear that this verse could be interpreted as lessening God's sovereignty: making people the determiners of when Christ will return. Such fears overlook the theme of *missio Dei*. God, who has always passionately sought the lost, has made humankind in His image able to serve as His agent in accomplishing His mission. As the Church moves to complete God's agenda of bringing salvation (2 Pet. 3:15) to the perishing, it demonstrates God's compassion (v. 9)—which will be satisfied before God closes this age.

At the same time, scoffing about Christ's "delay" is predicted (see 2 Pet. 3:3–4). In this context believers are urged to live holy lives "as [they] look forward to the day of God and speed its coming" (3:12). Since the delay has just been linked to prolonged opportunity for repentance, "speed[ing] its coming" must relate in some way to the ingathering of the souls for whom the Lord patiently waits.[1] This passage thus corresponds with Christ's teaching that the end will follow the proclamation of the gospel as a witness to all nations (Matt. 24:14; Mark 13:10).

The epistles of John hold out for correct doctrine and righteous living in view of blatant challenges to both. The answer to these challenges is seen in keeping one-self from the world while at the same time ministering to the world. In an important verse for the theme of missions, 1 John 2:2 states, "He is the atoning sacrifice for our sins, and not only for ours but also for the sins of the whole world" (Gk. *kosmou*). In another reference

---

[1]For further reading, see the helpful notes on 2 Pet. 3:12 in Donald C. Stamps, ed., *The Full Life Study Bible* (Grand Rapids: Zondervan Publishing House, 1992), 1970; and in Kenneth L. Barker, ed., *The NIV Study Bible* (Grand Rapids: Zondervan Publishing House, 1985), 1903.

using *kosmou*, 1 John 4:14 states: "We have seen and testify that the Father has sent his Son to be the Savior of the world." These words, once the Samaritan confession (John 4:42), are now used as the confession of the Church.

Revelation

Finally, in the Book of Revelation, Jesus reveals to John the completion of the long journey to the "ends of the earth."

First, the Kingdom motif so dominant in the Old Testament and the Gospels is invoked throughout the book: For example, the throne is mentioned in Revelation 1:4 and becomes a dominant theme. John refers to believers as both a "kingdom and priests" in 1:6, a theme expanded in 5:9–10: "They sang a new song: 'You are worthy to take the scroll and to open its seals, because you were slain, and with your blood you purchased men for God from every tribe and language and people and nation. You have made them to be a kingdom and priests to serve our God, and they will reign on the earth.' "

In these verses, it is a blood-bought people from every tribe, language, people, and nation who are first identified as a kingdom and priests and who then reign with Christ. Before the conclusion of salvation history, the priestly mission that God gave the people of Israel in Exodus 19:5–6 will have become universal: The *missio Dei* will have become *from* all nations *to* all nations. Those thus having represented the kingdom of Christ in its suffering phase will then represent the kingdom of Christ in its ruling phase. In a final reference to this theme, Revelation 20:6 states that those who are part of the "first resurrection" will be "priests of God and of Christ" and will "reign with him for a thousand years." The reference to reigning completes the kingdom concept typically associated with the priestly function of the people of God.

The seven churches addressed in chapters 2 and 3 are

in the province of Asia and thus may be said to be "missions churches." It is significant that the drama of the Apocalypse unfolds before the churches in the mission field of the first century: The churches being urged to love, to obey, to repent, to endure persecution even through martyrdom, and to do heroic deeds are the churches of what had recently been considered the frontier of the gospel. This phenomenon illustrates the full integration of every new people into the drama of redemption.

In the midst of this Church expansion, the Lord speaks to the church in Thyatira (2:26): "To him who overcomes and does my will to the end, I will give authority over the nations." Christ's will specifically included His church's resisting pagan influences, both immediate and remote in time, so as to remain His church among the nations, over whom it was destined to rule.

By repeatedly listing the people of the world, John indicates that the battle between the kingdoms of light and darkness also involves all peoples. Those redeemed by the Lamb's blood are said to be from " 'every tribe and language and people and nation' " (5:9). Again, in 7:9 the great multitude is from every "nation, tribe, people and language." Later, the Beast was given authority over "every tribe, people, language and nation" (13:7). Then, an angel preaches the eternal gospel "to those who live on the earth—to every nation, tribe, language and people" (14:6).

An abundance of royal titles begin in Revelation 1:5, where Christ is called the "ruler of the kings of the earth." In 3:7, as the holder of the " 'key of David,' " He opens and shuts the doors of opportunity at his pleasure. A few verses later (v. 14), Christ is referred to as " 'the ruler of God's creation.' " Then in 3:21, it is the one who overcomes to whom He says, "'I will give the right to sit with me on my throne, just as I overcame and sat down with my Father on his throne.'" As pointed out in chapter 3, John's Gospel recorded Jesus transferring

His apostleship to the disciples (John 20:21). The association with Christ now goes beyond the stage of work, suffering, and martyrdom and into the stage of kingdom victory and authority. Those faithful in this life will rule with Christ in the next. It is the Lion of Judah, the Root of David, who is able to open the seals (Rev. 5:5). Revelation 11:15 announces Christ's final accomplishment of His mission: " 'The kingdom of the world has become the kingdom of our Lord and of his Christ, and he will reign for ever and ever.' " No wonder the mighty rider on the white horse has this name written: "KING OF KINGS AND LORD OF LORDS" (19:16).

The promise plan of God is thus concluded in a grand note of triumph. The twin themes of blessing the nations (Gen. 12:3 et al.) and the eternal kingdom (2 Sam. 7:16 et al.) are united in all nations worshipping the eternal King, Christ himself.

The single promise plan evident throughout both Old and New Testaments will be accomplished by the power of God working primarily in and through His church. Even so, come Lord Jesus.

STUDY QUESTIONS

1. Evaluate the contributions of Hebrews and of James to the theme of *missio Dei*.
2. How are the "elect strangers" of 1 Peter 1:1 an example of the progress of God's plan within the New Testament era?
3. Explain the "speed its coming" reference of 2 Peter 3:12, relating it to biblical antecedents or parallel texts, including Matthew 24:14.
4. In what ways do the epistles of John advance the theme of a single worldwide plan of salvation?
5. Explain how the "kingdom of priests" motif (Exod. 19:6) comes to a conclusion in the Book of Revelation.
6. How does Revelation conclude the familiar themes of "all nations" and "kingdom"?

UNIT 2:
MISSIONS THROUGH THE CENTURIES

Two flawed approaches to missions are common in our day. Some follow the streams of missions tradition so closely that there is little creative thinking, little tolerance for change, and the traditions of the past are allowed to define the future. Others approach missions as entrepreneurs and pragmatists with little regard for the past. At times, this latter group views missions with an attitude bordering on arrogance. A particular revival movement or mission endeavor, for example, is viewed as though it were virtually the first manifestation of redemptive activity since the time of the apostles.

How are these extremes to be avoided? This unit encourages analyzing the major paradigms of missions history with the intent of projecting outcomes of a given missions practice.

The view taken throughout the unit is that a Pentecostal missions paradigm will contribute most effectively to the accomplishment of *missio Dei* if it sees itself in relationship to the historic development of missions. Pentecostals should understand their movement's continuity and discontinuity with missions of previous eras. As they understand the missions dynamics of the apostolic, medieval, reformation, and present eras, the authenticity of the past and the challenges of the present will synergize as missions in the age of the Spirit.

Chapter 6:

Approaching Missions History

The New Testament closes with the Early Church on the move: proclaiming Jesus as Lord and Christ everywhere, discipling new believers, and bearing the persecution of both religion and state while awaiting His return.

The Gospels give a uniform witness that Jesus left His followers with both a command that they make disciples among all nations and a promise that He would return. The command to make disciples and the promise to return were both set in the context of His kingdom. That Kingdom had already appeared in the person of Jesus of Nazareth, Messiah and King, yet it was still to appear in its fullness. In fact, the kingly authority of the risen Christ was the basis for the commissioning of His disciples to make yet more disciples—among all nations. Further He assured them that His manifest presence would accompany the completion of this Kingdom " 'to the very end of the age' " (Matt. 28:20).

Mark closes with the disciples going everywhere in obedience to Christ's injunction to " 'Go into all the world and preach the good news to all creation' " (Mark 16:15). From His seat at the right hand of God, "The Lord worked with them and confirmed His word by the signs that accompanied it" (Mark 16:20).

Luke records that after Jesus rose from the dead, He opened their minds to understand the witness of the Old Testament Scriptures concerning three things: His having to suffer, His rising from the dead, and their needing to preach repentance and forgiveness of sins in His name " 'beginning at Jerusalem' " (Luke 24:47; cf. vv. 45–46). "On this occasion Jesus went beyond showing how prophecy was fulfilled in His passion and resurrection. It was also fulfilled in the preaching of *repentance and forgiveness of sins.*"[1] This agrees with the records of the Old Testament. In various psalms, for example, and in the second part of Isaiah, it is clearly prophesied that the ultimate purpose of the divine revelation was that the glad tidings of salvation be brought to all peoples.[2]

The modern Christian may be inclined to ignore the Church that existed between the New Testament era as described by Luke and a more recent era: for example, the Protestant Reformation of the sixteenth century or the Pentecostal revival of the early twentieth century or a more recent phenomena such as a revival or the planting and growth of a specific national or local church. Those who begin their consideration of missions at such reference points tend to ignore the working of God in the world throughout the entire history of the Church.

There are problems with such approaches. To begin with, to suppose that God left the world essentially without witness at some point is without substantiation either in biblical prophecy or recorded history. Another problem with such an approach is that by limiting the consideration of the past Church, the present Church seriously disadvantages itself in accomplishing its biblical mission. Through consideration of the past we learn both positive and negative lessons about the

---

[1]Leon Morris, *Luke*, rev. ed., vol. 3 of *Tyndale New Testament Commentaries*, ed. Leon Morris (Grand Rapids: Wm. B. Eerdmans, 1992), 374, Morris's emphasis.
[2]Norval Geldenhuys, *The Gospel of Luke*, in *The New International Commentary on the New Testament*, ed. F. F. Bruce (Grand Rapids: Wm. B. Eerdmans, 1993), 641.

role of the Church within its immediate setting, or environment, with respect to its mission to the world at large, and even with respect to its doctrine and internal polity.

Paradigms

One way to approach missions history is to group significant events into time periods, paying special attention to the controlling motif, or set of assumptions, characteristic of each time period. Missiologist David J. Bosch, following Hans Kung, referred to these characteristic assumptions as "paradigms"[3] and grouped them as follows:

1. The apocalyptic paradigm of primitive Christianity.
2. The Hellenistic paradigm of the patristic period.
3. The medieval Roman Catholic paradigm.
4. The Protestant (Reformation) paradigm.
5. The modern Enlightenment paradigm.
6. The emerging ecumenical paradigm.[4]

Analyzing these paradigms and approaching the present task with an understanding of historical precedent may assist the Church in its task today.

We can recognize paradigms by noting how the Church of any period has defined its purpose and approached its mission. Though the identification of cause and effect is complex, we can recognize trends

---

[3]The concepts of *paradigm* and *paradigm shift* are usually credited to Thomas Kuhn and his *Structure of Scientific Revolutions* (see Lawrence T. McHargue, "The Christian and Natural Science," in *Elements of a Christian Worldview*, ed. Michael D. Palmer [Springfield, Mo.: Logion Press, 1998], 170).

[4]David J. Bosch, *Transforming Mission: Paradigm Shifts in Theology of Mission* (Maryknoll, N.Y.: Orbis Books, 1991), 181–89. Bosch, in turn, credits Hans Kung for the development of these categories. Note with respect to his sixth paradigm that Bosch ignores conservative evangelical and Pentecostal resistance to ecumenism, the relative ineffectiveness of the liberal ecumenical movement, and the growth of Pentecostal missions in recent times.

and relate them to the belief and practice of the church in question. We must also consider the relationship of Church to state and society, since the Church exists within a wider environment. The Church's relationship to government, its acceptance or rejection of current social norms, and the degree to which it assimilates popular notions of philosophy and religion will all affect its sense of mission.

Viewed this way, each historical period is something of a missions laboratory. The researcher finds enough data to indicate the Church's perception of its mission and how that perception affected those professing to be Christian. This data may include records concerning doctrine, the Church's understanding of its role within society, the Church's understanding of its mission, and the influence of changing political landscapes. The objective is to suggest cause-effect phenomena. Viewed in this way, the student sets up a two-part hypothesis:

1. When the Church
   believed a certain doctrine, or
   practiced a certain method of expansion, or
   viewed life in a certain way, or
   lived under a certain form of church or civil government,

2. then the Church
   grew rapidly, or
   failed to grow, or
   became syncretistic, or
   deepened in piety and biblical purpose.

How, then, does a student go about making such observations? Kenneth Scott Latourette has suggested seven questions to be asked of each time period with respect to the expansion of the Church. Consideration of these questions will help the *when* observations to be seen in relationship to the *then* outcomes. Latourette's questions are as follows:

1. What was the Christianity that spread?
2. Why did Christianity spread?
3. Why has Christianity suffered reverses, and at times met only partial successes?
4. By what processes did Christianity spread?
5. What effect has Christianity had upon its environment?
6. What effect has the environment had upon Christianity?
7. What bearing do the processes by which Christianity spread have upon the effect of Christianity on its environment, and of the environment upon Christianity?[5]

Learning from the Paradigms

In the modern era until the late twentieth century, the vast majority of missions energy has flowed from the West to the non-Western, or Two-Thirds, world. Because of this, it has been natural for new missions agencies, whether from the West or from the Two-Thirds World, to regard the paradigms of the recent Western past as standards. However, by using questions such as Latourette's to reflect upon historical paradigms, the student will gain a wider view of missions models. From them, missions planners may also gain insight for shaping appropriate models for contemporary missionary endeavors. This is especially important for both non-Western practitioners of missions and those who may train them. At the same time, those who are developing missions models should not allow themselves to be limited by the models they are studying. Rather, such models should be used only as a starting place from which both synthesis and new models may develop.

---

[5]Kenneth Scott Latourette, *A History of the Expansion of Christianity* (New York: Harper & Brothers, 1937), 1:x–xv.

Both positive and negative factors of historical paradigms should inform one's approach to missions. Latourette's seven questions should be a means toward the definition of missionary paradigms. The diversity of the Church's answers to these questions over the centuries identifies change in how the Church perceived and practiced missions. The student's objective should be to recognize the historical approaches to missions, including the resulting strengths and weaknesses of each approach. This will help the student foresee likely outcomes of present or projected missionary strategies.

Although this outline will touch each paradigm Bosch and Kung have suggested, it will do so following Latourette's grouping of events in three major time periods.

The outline will be as follows:

Period	Date	Major Descriptors of Paradigms
Period 1	The Early Church to A.D. 500	Apostolic, Apocalyptic, Spontaneous, Hellenistic
Period 2	A.D. 500–1500	Medieval Roman Catholic
Period 3	A.D. 1500–2000	Reformation, Enlightenment, Ecumenical, Evangelical, Pentecostal

While not following Latourette's seven questions serially, these should be viewed as informing considerations in the summaries that I present.

STUDY QUESTIONS

1. Give the three major points Luke records as Jesus' postresurrection teaching from the Old Testament.
2. What problems result from ignoring the lessons of church history?
3. What questions does Latourette suggest we should ask to gain an understanding of the expansion of Christianity within each period of missions history?

Chapter 7:

The Apostolic Church and Mission

Period 1:
The Early Church to A.D. *500, Apostolic,*
Apocalyptic, Spontaneous, Hellenistic

The first period of missions history began with the work of the apostles and the churches of their period. David J. Bosch identifies the period as the apocalyptic paradigm of the primitive, or Early, Church. Unquestionably the Early Church saw a connection between their mission and the return of Jesus Christ. Jesus himself taught this connection in such verses as Matthew 24:14: " 'This gospel of the kingdom will be preached in the whole world as a testimony to all nations, and then the end will come.' " His ascension followed His promise that the disciples would receive power to bear witness of Him " 'to the ends of the earth' " (Acts 1:8). Immediately after the ascension, the angels inquired, " 'Men of Galilee . . . why do you stand here looking into the sky? This same Jesus, who has been taken from you into heaven, will come back in the same way you have seen him go into heaven' " (Acts 1:11). The apostles uniformly taught the new churches that Jesus would return soon (e.g., 1 Thess.; 2 Pet. 3, et al.). Though Jesus was returning soon, apparent delay would bring scoffers (2 Pet. 3:3–7); while the Church was to evangelize the world in view of Jesus' coming, it was also to remain holy as the people of God Jesus was coming for (2 Pet. 3:11–12).

This apocalyptic atmosphere characterized both the motivation and a good deal of the message of the apostles and other believers as the Church grew with great spontaneity during the early era. Within the apostolic period a major purpose of organizing the new churches was to incorporate them into the ongoing task of expansion—all in an atmosphere expecting the imminent return of Christ. As Stephen Neill summarizes, "As soon as a church had taken root under its local leaders, Paul felt free to move onward towards a further fulfillment of His plan, that all the Gentiles might hear the word of the Lord and so the end might come."[1] Paul could move on as he did largely because he saw his task as being the establishment of churches that were what we now call "indigenous." They did not have to identify with the missionaries in such cultural matters as language and dress, and they had no financial dependence upon the missionaries.[2]

External Challenge

Periodic persecution also marked this period until the legalization of Christianity under Constantine in A.D. 313. At first, Roman persecution tended to be localized. For example, the notorious persecution under Nero, brutal though it was, did not lead to persecution beyond Rome.[3] Later, Christians were less protected, and persecution increased under such emperors as Marcus Aurelius (161–180), Decius (249–251), and Valerian (253–260). The most widespread and severe persecution of this period broke out under Diocletian on February 23, A.D. 303. Though he abdicated two years

[1]Stephen Neill, *A History of Christian Missions,* rev. ed. (London: Penguin Books, 1984), 27.
[2]Ralph D. Winter, "The Kingdom Strikes Back," in *Perspectives On The World Christian Movement,* ed. Ralph D. Winter and Steven C. Hawthorne, rev. ed. (Pasadena: William Carey Library, 1993), B-8.
[3]Howard F. Vos, *Exploring Church History* (Nashville: Thomas Nelson, 1994), 27.

later, the persecution itself lasted ten years.[4] Although many were killed and others denied the faith, the picture of the Church prior to Constantine is most notable for its seemingly unstoppable expansion and apocalyptic mindset. In pointing out the tendency of later generations to idealize and exaggerate this persecution, Neill nonetheless notes: "Every Christian knew that sooner or later he might have to testify to his faith at the cost of his life."[5] Christ and the apostles had often foretold persecution before the end, and the martyrdoms were seen in this light—as indications of the nearness of Christ's return.

Internal Challenge

Challenges to the Church's mission also came from inside the Church itself. Many of the doctrinal aberrations that arose came from the contact the Church had with its pagan Greco-Roman environment. Pagan religious thought was often at variance from the central Christian belief of the incarnation of God in the person of Jesus Christ. Incipient Gnosticism, opposed in such New Testament passages as Philippians 2:5–11, Colossians 1:15–20, and 1 John 4:1–3, became a full-blown, frontal attack by the second century. Whereas Paul had insisted, in his primitive "kerygma,"[6] upon the centrality of Christ's incarnation, death, and resurrection and John had anathematized any who denied that "Christ [had] come in the flesh," in time a range of destructive heresies, predicted by the apostles (i.e., 2 Tim. 3:1–9,13), surfaced in the church.

Whether in its incipient or more developed forms, Gnosticism postulated a dualism that said spirit was good and matter was evil. This led some to deny the

---

[4]Harry R. Boer, *A Short History of the Early Church* (Grand Rapids: Wm. B. Eerdmans, 1976), 102–3.
[5]Neill, *Christian Missions*, 38.
[6]"Early preaching," a term used for passages such as 1 Cor. 15:1–8.

incarnation of Christ. They reasoned that God as spirit was too good to have become matter, that is, flesh. They taught the existence of a series of emanations between earth and heaven. This gave rise to the veneration of angels as being more nearly spirit and thus better than humanity. They spoke of Jesus Christ as only having *seemed* human (a teaching that came to be called docetism, from the Gk. *dokein*, "to seem").[7]

Gnostics tended toward extremes in behavior as well. In an effort to deny the flesh, some became radically ascetic. Others became sensual, claiming either that satiation of the flesh would somehow lead to its destruction or that the flesh was simply not real and therefore didn't matter. Those who mixed Gnosticism with Christianity rejected much of Scripture and denied the incarnation of Christ. They called the God of the Old Testament a Demiurge, different from the God in the New Testament, and extreme forms of both asceticism and sensuality developed.

Such a Hellenized Christianity could not retain the missionary fervor of New Testament Christianity. At the same time, it proved attractive to Greeks, gaining many adherents. But Gnosticism was so fundamentally different that its spread represented an affront to Christianity. Nevertheless, it continued to select and develop ideas from Christ's teachings, viewing them as a means of overcoming the "evil" physical world and entering into Light. Church members influenced by such teachings came to regard salvation as being gained by faith and works, all of which they celebrated as great mystery. Gnosticism did not last long as a supposed form of Christian worship; nevertheless it left a legacy of asceticism and a pronounced dichotomy between clergy and laity.[8] But ultimately Christian

[7]David J. Bosch, *Transforming Mission: Paradigm Shifts in Theology of Mission* (Maryknoll, N.Y.: Orbis Books, 1991), 200.
[8]Vos, *Exploring Church History*, 32.

apologists refuted it, and the Church of the post-Gnostic era remained committed to orthodoxy.[9]

Another challenge came in the form of Ebionism, an early continuation of a radical Jewish legalism, which was opposed by the apostle Paul. To the Ebionites, salvation was by works, Christ was not divine, and Paul's writings were not Scripture.[10]

During its first two centuries and into the third, the Church retained an openness to prophetic ministry. Asterius Urbanus, Irenaeus, and Eusebius are all cited as early authorities stating that the mainline church into the early third century expected prophecy to continue until the Second Coming (Gk. *parousia*).[11] A notable charismatic movement, the Montanists, arose in the mid-second century in central Asia Minor. They were condemned by several church synods amid allegations of error, especially with respect to prophecy, and the Church reacted by declaring that both biblical revelation and spiritual gifts were no longer possible.[12] Nonetheless, this group is regarded as having been generally orthodox.[13] Its most famous convert, the polemicist Tertullian of Carthage, is sometimes regarded as the father of Roman Catholic theology. His famous exposition of the doctrine of the Trinity, *Against Praxeas,* is dated about A.D. 210, whereas his conversion to Montanism is dated 207.[14] What the Montanists really believed is difficult to ascertain because what is known about them comes mostly from their opponents and because of changes within the movement after the

---

[9]Bosch, *Transforming Mission,* 200.

[10]Vos, *Exploring Church History,* 31; see also J. F. Bethune-Baker, *An Introduction to the Early History of Christian Doctrine* (London: Methuen, 1903), 63–68.

[11]Stanley M. Burgess, *The Spirit & the Church: Antiquity* (Peabody, Mass.: Hendrickson Publishers, 1984), 51.

[12]Vos, *Exploring Church History,* 33.

[13]Ibid.

[14]Ibid., 18; Boer, *Early Church,* 64.

deaths of its founders. Even though it was condemned, Montanism stands as an indication of the continued desire for charismatic manifestation into the third century.

The first period of missions expansion should be regarded as the most characteristically Pentecostal period until the modern era. The Church's growth was directly related to its Pentecostal experience. As Bosch comments, "The significance for the early Christian mission up to the third century of charismatic healer-missionaries, miracle workers, and itinerant preachers should not be underestimated."[15]

V. Raymond Edman identifies three major factors in the growth of the Church during this period: the effectiveness of the early prophets, the effectiveness of teachers, and the changed lives and testimony of women.[16]

Although the function of prophets was greatly curtailed after the suppression of the Montanists, prophets were a significant factor during the formative centuries of the Church. These early prophets seem to have been inspired preachers who expounded the truths of the gospel, often with special insights given through the Holy Spirit. Enough of these prophets were itinerant to require regulation of their activities at the time of the second century *Didache* (or "Teaching").[17] In time, their function largely gave way to local bishops, around which a church centered. The bishops strengthened the churches, but the rise of their influence often coincided with the decline of the prophetic gifts.

---

[15]Bosch, *Transforming Mission*, 191.

[16]V. Raymond Edman, *The Light in Dark Ages* (Wheaton, Ill.: Van Kampen Press, 1949), 34–35.

[17]Ibid., 6, 34. *The Didache* ("The Teaching of Lord to the Gentiles Through the Twelve Apostles") enumerated ecclesiastical policies, e.g., regulating baptism and communion, as well as moral instruction.

Jewish tradition taught that "respect for a teacher should surpass that for a father, for son and father alike owe respect to a teacher."[18] This influenced the Early Church to regard teachers highly. They came to function as non-elected, local servants of the church. This contrasted with bishops, who were elected, and with prophets, who were often itinerant.

The Gospels abound with accounts of ministry by and to women. This pattern carried over into Acts and the Epistles. Edman writes, "Paganism had degraded woman, reducing her to slavery, dependency, vanity: the gospel had elevated her to her rightful place, for in Christ there is 'neither male nor female.' "[19] Besides their daily testimony and service, Christian women often sealed such ministry with their blood, for they too were singled out in the periodic persecutions. Neill mentions female martyrs such as the wealthy Perpetua and her slave girl Felicitas, who died together in Carthage in A.D. 203. He observes, "There is no doubt that the attitude of the martyrs, and particularly of the young women who suffered along with the men, made a deep impression."[20]

Christianity grew by its very nature. Neill says, "What is clear is that every Christian was a witness. Where there were Christians, there would be a living, burning faith, and before long an expanding Christian community."[21] It should be recognized, however, that there were also full-time workers, such as Paul and his helpers, and that churches supported these workers financially.[22] This basic approach of an organized missionary team was borrowed from the Pharisees (but see Matt. 23:15).[23] The Church's inherent missionary nature

[18]Ibid., 34.
[19]Ibid., 35.
[20]Neill, *Christian Missions,* 38; see also 34, 37.
[21]Ibid., 22.
[22]Ibid., 21–22.
[23]Winter, "Kingdom Strikes Back," B-8.

combined with the strategic advances of full-time workers yielded the growth of its first three centuries.

The Church of this era expected Christ to return in its lifetime, emphasized experiential religion, and aggressively proclaimed Christ. In addition to validation by miracles, this proclamation was validated by the love and personal holiness of its adherents. Those tired of moral laxity were attracted to the higher moral standard of the Christians.

Both friendly and unfriendly sources attest this success of the Church in the immediate period after the apostles. From inside the Church itself, the epistles of Ignatius are an early evidence of this success. Ignatius was bishop of Antioch in Syria and wrote seven letters on his way to martyrdom in Rome in about A.D. 110. The letters show that the development of the Church around local bishops was common at this time.[24] From a hostile source, Pliny the Younger, comes similar evidence of Church growth. In about 112, he wrote the Roman Emperor Trajan asking what to do with the growing Christian menace.[25] These opponents "frequently mentioned the extraordinary conduct of Christians, often with reference to the fact that this conduct had been a factor in winning people over to the Christian faith."[26]

After the destruction of Jerusalem in A.D. 70, the center of Christianity shifted to Antioch of Syria. From there Paul and Barnabas had set out on their first missionary journey and then returned there at the journey's end. By the time of John Chrysostom, at the end of the fourth century, fully half of Antioch's population of 500,000 was said to be Christian.[27] In the course of time, other places became major centers of Christian

---

[24]Neill, *Christian Missions*, 28.
[25]Ibid.
[26]Bosch, *Transforming Mission*, 192.
[27]Neill, *Christian Missions*, 29.

activity, including Rome and Alexandria, Egypt.

Estimates of the numerical strength of the Church by the end of the third century vary greatly, depending upon how empire-wide projections are developed from available local data and the writing of the apologists. They indicate that the percentage of the population that was Christian in the East was much higher than in the West. J. Herbert Kane cites estimates of 50 million to 100 million believers and feels this could have been as much as ten percent of the population.[28]

As time passed, the Church came to an increasing accommodation of the delay of the Second Coming and began to centralize and institutionalize. Subsequent revival movements, even if aberrations, bear witness to the perception that there was a pristine period of God's blessing which needed to be restored. It was the fire of this earlier period that attracted converts. Even when the fire burned low, enough of its essential message remained to continue to attract them. The essential element of the message of the Church of this period was Christological. By A.D. 200, the candidate for baptism had to confess belief in these foundational truths concerning Christ: the incarnation of the Son of God, born of the Virgin Mary, crucified, resurrected, and coming again.[29] By the late fourth century, these beliefs had been combined with statements concerning both the Trinity and the Church and formalized into what was first known as the Roman Creed and has been subsequently known as the Apostles' Creed.[30]

With increased Hellenization and decreasing emphasis upon eschatological themes, the Church saw less

---

[28]J. Herbert Kane, *A Concise History of the Christian World Mission* (Grand Rapids: Baker Book House, 1982), 17; see also Neill, *Christian Missions,* 30–31, 39; Kenneth Scott Latourette, *A History of the Expansion of Christianity* (New York: Harper & Brothers, 1937), 1:169.

[29]Boer, *Short History,* 75–76.

[30]Ibid., 75–77.

significance in Paul's writings. When they were quoted, it was for an ethical sense, not for an eschatological
emphasis.[31] The Church's emphasis was more on har-
monizing Greek thought and Christ as *Logos* than on
His second advent and the inauguration of His future
kingdom. The apologists largely succeeded in defend-
ing the Church against a wholesale takeover by
Gnosticism; nonetheless the paradigm was being
changed. Instead of an apostolic apocalyptic paradigm
of mission, there came to be a philosophical understanding of reality. The Church remained for the most
part orthodox, but the battle for faith was fought within the bounds of Greek philosophical thought rather
than within the framework of the primitive apostolic
faith. Thus, even the victories of the apologists herald-
ed a new era characterized by a Hellenistic paradigm.
Changes were gradual rather than abrupt. And mission, for many who retained orthodox faith, became
more associated with the development of a philosophical
rationale for faith in Christ than with the spontaneous
expansion of the Church as a herald of His imminent
return.

The positive side of Greek influence may be seen in
the use of Greek throughout the Roman Empire. As
Stephen Neill notes, "The Roman Empire had accepted
Greek both as the language of trade and as the medium
of familiar intercourse between all educated men."[32] Its
widespread use both facilitated communication and
the use, as early as Paul, of multiethnic evangelistic
teams. Even the church at Rome, although it touched
the highest echelons of society, was primarily a church
of the common classes—as is evidenced by its use of
Greek rather than Latin for at least its first century of
existence.[33]

---

[31]Ibid., 196.
[32]Neill, *Christian Missions*, 25.
[33]Ibid., 30.

The greatest reason for the remarkable growth of the Church during these centuries, as Kenneth Scott Latourette observes, was Jesus himself. "It was because of what Jesus did to His intimates and because of their belief in Him and in His death, resurrection, and early return that Christianity set out upon its career of conquest."[34] Other reasons often cited include its organization into a closely knit community, the eventual favor of the state, the void created by the disintegration of society, and its appeal to so many diverse elements of the population (all races and languages, rich and poor, all social classes, both sexes). Even though it was strongly dependent upon its Jewish roots, the Church was able to answer the philosophical questions of the day. It presented a gospel of power, both over the sinful tendencies of the flesh and over sickness and evil spirits.

The Church during the apocalyptic era of its first centuries may be characterized as believing the doctrines of the Scriptures as summarized in the creeds that emerged during this time. It saw itself as a witnessing community, announcing the news of Christ's kingdom and calling the nations to repentance before Christ's return. As Neill observes, "The church was the body of Christ, indwelt by His Spirit; and what Christ had begun to do, that the Church would continue to do, through all the days and unto the uttermost parts of the earth until His unpredictable but certain coming again."[35]

With the growth of Christianity came social reform, even while the Church was discouraged from becoming politically active by its lack of legal standing (i.e., before Constantine the Great adopted it). From this remarkable beginning, the Church was about to enter centuries marked by turmoil, the impact of a non-Christian environment, and the effects of its alliance with the state. The next chapter will discuss this.

---

[34]Latourette, *History of the Expansion,* 1:170.
[35]Neill, *Christian Missions,* 23.

STUDY QUESTIONS

1. Explain what is meant in Bosch's characterization of the first 500 years as the apocalyptic paradigm. How did the Early Church's eschatological understanding affect its sense of mission?
2. Summarize the effect of persecution upon the expansion of the Church during this first period.
3. What was the effect of the doctrinal challenges that arose during the first 500 years from within the Church?
4. Comment on the significance of prophetic manifestations and miracles within this period.
5. Explain the assertion, "Christianity grew by its very nature."
6. Comment on the significance of the high code of moral conduct among Christians within the first period as it relates to the expansion of Christianity.
7. What changes came to the Church's understanding of its mission in consequence of the delay of the *parousia* and the increasing Hellenization of the Church?
8. Evaluate the reasons given for the growth of the Church within its first 500 years. Consider the existence or lack of parallels within the church of your experience today, and comment on how these similarities or lack of similarities may be affecting the Church's current rate of expansion.
9. Before the time of Constantine, what was the role of the Church in lobbying for social reform? State this role in terms of a "when/then" construction with respect to both the expansion of the Church and the reforming influence of the Church within society. Do you feel there is a basis for forming an "if/then" hypothesis with respect to today's church where you live?

Chapter 8:
De-emphasizing
Missio Dei

Period 2:
A.D. *500–1500, Medieval Roman Catholic*

Legalizing Christianity

With Rome's legalizing Christianity in A.D. 313 and then elevating it to the status of state religion, the Church was no longer persecuted. For the first time its eschatological significance was no longer confirmed by outside forces, that is, persecution. As a result the Church lessened its emphasis on Christ's return. Though the doctrine itself was never repudiated, de-emphasizing it had the effect of de-emphasizing *missio Dei*.

The Hellenistic influence of the earlier centuries continued into the medieval period. The Eastern Church seemed particularly fond of doctrinal controversy, and many of the issues they debated reflected Greek influence. One such area of Greek influence that carried over into the Roman, or Latin, Church was the dualistic mindset that spirit is good and flesh is bad. This rejection of the material world figured prominently in monasticism and the entire medieval Church. In 1074, for example, Gregory VII banned all clerical marriage.[1] Though his motives may have included the making of a nonhereditary priesthood loyal to the papacy, the influence of Gnostic (Greek) thought concerning the evil of the flesh is readily apparent.

---

[1]Howard F. Vos, *Exploring Church History* (Nashville: Thomas Nelson, 1994), 65.

With the growing popularity of the Church following the legalization of Christianity, spiritually unregen-
erate people swelled its ranks. That is not to say that no
growth in this period was genuine, but there is little
evidence that genuineness of saving faith was typical.
Through its pagan associations, primitive Christianity
had changed in such areas as holidays, moral standards, prevailing forms of church government, and
sense of mission.

Another result of the legalizing of Christianity was the
direct entry of emperors into the affairs of the church.
For example, Constantine was not baptized until on his
deathbed;[2] nevertheless, he presided over several church
councils called to settle significant theological issues. He
himself called the ecumenical council in Nicea in A.D.
325, which decided for the Athanasian rather than the
Arian position on the Trinity.[3] Given this precedent, in
431 Emperor Theodosius II called a council in Ephesus
to address the controversy over the nature of Christ
raised by Nestorius.[4] This decision was to have later significance in the spread of Christianity, for the banned
Nestorians went east to Central Asia and on to China in
the seventh century.[5] This mixing of the affairs of state
and church became the pattern for centuries to come. On
the one hand, emperors would see themselves as the

---

[2]His forgoing of baptism until his deathbed probably had little to
do with when or whether he was converted; rather, it was because
of his concern with having all of his sins forgiven through baptism.
[3]Despite the fact that Constantine favored the Arian view, which
treated Christ as a created being. See Kerry D. McRoberts, "The
Holy Trinity," in *Systematic Theology,* ed. Stanley M. Horton, rev. ed.
(Springfield, Mo.: Logion Press, 1995), 162–63.
[4]Nestorius presented Jesus "as the God-bearing man" with the
Logos indwelling "the human Jesus similarly to the way the Holy
Spirit indwells the believer." David R. Nichols, "The Lord Jesus
Christ," in *Systematic Theology,* ed. Horton, 311.
[5]Kenneth Scott Latourette, *A History of the Expansion of Christianity*
(New York: Harper & Brothers, 1937), 1:231; see also Vos, *Exploring
Church History,* 41.

head of everything, spiritual as well as secular. On the other hand, the bishop of Rome would often exercise civil as well as ecclesiastical control.

The struggle between heads of state and Church reached a peak during the "lay investiture controversy" of the eleventh century. Political leaders of Europe were accustomed to investing the top echelons of the clergy with both civil and religious authority. Pope Gregory VII (Hildebrand) challenged this procedure, provoking a bitter feud between the papacy and Henry IV, the Emperor of the Holy Roman Empire.[6] Gregory excommunicated Henry, and Henry countered by calling a synod of bishops in 1076 that deposed Gregory. Henry's nobles forced a reconciliation, vivid for Gregory's making Henry wait barefoot in the snow for three days before being received. Henry later set up another pope and Gregory died in exile, but the papacy ultimately won the investiture debate.[7]

Medieval Missions Paradigm

The period of the medieval Roman Church is too long and complex to characterize with a single paradigm. However, the form of Christianity that spread and the means by which it spread reveal recurrent and dominant features that may be considered as the medieval mission paradigm. Typical features of this

---

[6]The Holy Roman Empire, according to *The New International Dictionary of the Christian Church,* was "a political entity in Medieval Europe" that may be dated to Otto I (962) (although the precise term 'holy' was not used until 1157). Pope John XII, of questionable reputation, thought he had an ally in Otto, only to find his appointee a much better man than himself. Otto (dubbed "the Great" by history) wanted to clean up the Papal act. This rocky marriage of church and state ultimately amounted to "essentially a German institution," which was dissolved in 1806. Meanwhile, the Eastern Orthodox church, begun by Constantine when he moved from Rome to Byzantium, continued to develop separately.
[7]Vos, *Exploring Church History,* 65–66.

paradigm, as identified by David J. Bosch, are its changed context, the individualization of salvation, the institutionalizing of salvation, mission between church and state, indirect and direct missionary wars, colonialism and missions, and the mission of monasticism.[8] I will now turn to the consideration of these six features of the medieval missions paradigm.

CHANGED CONTEXT

The primary "changed context" of the medieval Roman church Bosch refers to is its transition from a Greek base to a Latin base. Among the many differences in orientation, the greatest was in its approach to salvation. Whereas the Greek-conditioned church had accepted the model of becoming a Christian through a training process, the Latin church, following Augustine of Hippo (A.D. 354–450), accepted the model of a crisis conversion.[9] This included Augustine's emphasis upon Pauline theology and his interpretation of Pauline teaching in such areas as original sin, predestination, and individual conversion. The effect was to stress "the individualization of salvation," not the redemption of the universe. The medieval Roman church saw sin as separating man from God, with Christ becoming flesh in order to provide for individual salvation. This emphasis led later generations into two major areas of debate: the meaning of election and the appropriate Christian response to the world. The emphasis upon soteriology, however, would remain a hallmark of Latin Christianity.

INDIVIDUAL SALVATION

The eventual resolution of another early controversy further supported the doctrine of individual salvation:

---

[8]David J. Bosch, *Transforming Mission: Paradigm Shifts in Theology of Mission* (Maryknoll, N.Y.: Orbis Books, 1991), 214–38.
[9]Ibid., 214–15.

The Donatist controversy arose after the ascendancy of Constantine brought an end to the previous emperor's persecution. Donatists, followers of Donatus, an early bishop of Carthage, regarded as apostate those clergy who had handed over their copies of Scripture during the persecution. When such a clergyman resumed his office, the Donatists held that any sacraments he performed were invalid, that some sins are unforgivable. Augustine stood strongly against the Donatists, holding that salvation was by grace and was therefore available even to those guilty of scandalous transgression.[10] The Donatists were powerful, but the views of Augustine eventually prevailed as the official view of the medieval church. Thus, the Church came to believe that salvation was an individual matter and that the basis of salvation was the grace of God.

A CENTRALIZATION OF POWER

Throughout the early centuries, the church underwent a gradual centralization of power. Cyprian's view, expressed in the mid-fourth century, that there was no salvation outside the church, became official dogma. The bishops became strong, and the bishop of Rome became a "first among equals," having great authority over the affairs of the Western church, over government in the Western Empire, and often over affairs even in Constantinople.[11] The adoption of Cyprian's view forged a close connection between salvation and the church; in practical terms, one's salvation became more a matter of one's relationship to the church than to

---

[10]Ibid., 218.

[11]Vos, *Exploring Church History*, 48–50. Emperor Constantine looked upon himself as God's representative on earth. So when he made Christianity the state religion, he presumed a role among the bishops of the Church. Thus when he relocated the capital of the Roman Empire to Byzantium in 330 (renaming it Constantinople), the Church essentially underwent a split, the bishop of Rome at this time becoming "first among equals."

Christ. And since baptism was the rite of initiation into the church, baptizing even the relatively uninformed resulted. Learning could come later, it was reasoned, if only salvation could be secured through entering the church by baptism. The task of mission, it followed, was to bring the pagan into the church through baptism.

The Church early left its Jewish heritage, embracing the Gentile, moving from Jerusalem to Antioch, eventually taking up the language of the Greeks. After settling in Rome, the organized church underwent another metamorphosis: adopting the Roman way of thinking and speaking. It now spoke Latin. But a further change in context came with the influx of barbarian tribes in the early fifth century. Though these barbarians would later destroy the Roman Empire, many became Christian and were for the most part respectful of the Church. Those whom Rome had been slack in sharing the gospel with, in time, became Rome's conquerors.[12] The same was true later when the Holy Roman Empire failed to win the Vikings. Those who were not evangelized came with a vengeance, wreaking havoc throughout the lands of those who could have evangelized them earlier. Unlike the Gothic barbarians, the Vikings had no respect for Christianity and took special delight in pillaging churches and monasteries and either killing the monks or selling them into slavery. In time, however, the invaders were Christianized. The point remains, however, that twice within the first twelve hundred years of the Church's history major destruction was visited upon its home base by those who could have been brought to faith in Christ had the church been missionary in its orientation.[13]

---

[12]Ralph D. Winter, "The Kingdom Strikes Back," in *Perspectives On The World Christian Movement*, ed. Ralph D. Winter and Steven C. Hawthorne, rev. ed. (Pasadena: William Carey Library, 1993), B-10–13.
[13]Ibid., B-13–16, B-20.

JOINT EFFORT OF CHURCH AND STATE

During this period missionary objectives were accomplished through the joint effort of Church and state. Once again, the basic background for this practice as it later developed came from the writings of Augustine. In his famous work, *City of God*, Augustine argued that spiritual power (the Church) was supreme over the power of the state. In later centuries, this led to the elevation of the papacy over the state, which in turn led to the utilization of the state as an agent of the Church's mission.

The medieval state came to see itself as an agent of the Church. The eventual effects of this teaching included both military conquest and, later, colonial expansion.

Augustine believed in nonviolent means for coercing heretics to come to repentance, including fines, confiscation of property, and exile.[14] He also believed in the concept of just warfare in cases of self-defense. But within two centuries, Gregory the Great included financial pressures and physical punishment in his coercive means to gain peasant conversion. In time, "indirect missionary war" was used to subjugate pagan peoples so that the missionaries might see to their conversion. Later, the distinction between "indirect war" and "direct war" was obscured as Charlemagne openly used military conquest to force the conversion of the Saxons.[15]

"MISSIONARY" WARS

The medieval period was a complex time with many conflicting dynamics. Charlemagne, for example, had a genuine interest in theology and strongly encouraged the development of centers of Christian scholarship. He

---

[14]Bosch, *Transforming Mission*, 223.
[15]Ibid., 114.

was the sole ruler of the Franks from A.D. 771 until 814 and was crowned Emperor of what became known as the Holy Roman Empire by Pope Leo II on Christmas day, 800. His methods of conversion reflect the prevailing idea of his time. Church and state accomplished mission through both "indirect and direct missionary wars." The conquest of pagan peoples was followed by forced conversion to Christianity. As Stephen Neill summarizes, "Once a German tribe had been conquered, its conversion was included in the terms of peace, as the price to be paid for enjoying the protection of the emperor and the good government that his arms ensured. But this meant an association of the new religion with the conquering power that could only be dangerous."[16]

Christian missionaries followed the armies of conquest, and displeasure with the rule of Charlemagne typically involved retaliation against these missionaries. Remarkably, their martyrdom did little to slow the advance of Christianity, as reinforcements invariably arrived to take their place. So in the matter of a few years, the cycle of conquering, sending of missionaries, martyrdom, reinforcement by more missionaries, more revolt and martyrdom, and yet more missionaries gradually led to the Christianization of the Saxons. Neill concludes, "With the process of time, the missionaries won their way. Resistance to the Gospel grew weaker, and by the time of the death of Charlemagne the pacification and conversion of the Saxons were reckoned to be complete."[17]

Even though conquest was used to Christianize others outside Germany (e.g., Norway and the Elbe Wends), the "direct missionary war" remained the exception. The concept that the "just war" was defen-

---

[16]Stephen Neill, *A History of Christian Missions,* rev. ed. (London: Penguin Books, 1984), 68.
[17]Ibid., 69.

sive in nature coupled with the incongruity of war as a means of evangelism kept war from becoming the typical means of Christianization.[18] It should be obvious that this is not an acceptable model of missions.

In the Crusades, though Christian armies attacked Muslims, the immediate objective was usually the recapturing of Jerusalem or other holy places, and the broader objective was the containment of Islam. The Crusades were not intended to make converts to Christianity and, therefore, should not be connected with missions.[19] This is not to say that those involved in the Crusades did not see their role as being one of mission. Rather, it is an observation that they made little attempt to gain converts by either persuasion or force. It has often been observed that many of the crusaders were devout. But "[t]he great lesson of the Crusades is that good will, even sacrificial obedience to God, is no substitute for a clear understanding of His will."[20] The Crusades failed in their objectives and caused great damage to Constantinople and the entire Eastern Church.

COLONIALISM AND MISSION

Colonialism and mission were closely related. The empire founded by Charlemagne lasted in some form for a thousand years. Part of the legacy it left for the European colonial era was the understanding that the peoples of a country were to share the religion of their sovereign.[21] First Catholic and later Protestant colonial expansion thus served the interests of both state and Church. Before the Protestant era, when Spain and

---

[18]Bosch, *Transforming Mission*, 224–25.
[19]Ibid., 225.
[20]Winter, "Kingdom Strikes Back," B-16.
[21]This was not a new idea. It has been an almost universal idea that only modern secularism has challenged. For Christ's kingdom to be universal, this view must be rejected.

Portugal were the dominant colonial powers, the Roman Catholic practice of patronage held that those with the right to colonize had the duty to Christianize.[22] In time, the concept of missions came to be understood as the Christianizing of the peoples within the various European nations' colonial spheres. As a consequence Christianity has been rejected by many.

THE PARADIGM OF MONASTIC MISSIONS

The mission of monasticism was extremely important during the medieval period. Early monasticism in the Eastern Church often took the form of individuals who rejected the world and lived isolated lives in quest of holiness and escape from the evil world. Western expressions of monasticism, by contrast, were largely communal. As the Roman Empire collapsed and the spiritual level of the Church declined, the monasteries flourished. They provided a place where the devout could leave an unhappy world and concentrate on spiritual issues, primarily upon attaining salvation. The monasteries often became centers of learning, where scrolls were copied, where sacred as well as secular learning was kept alive during hostile times. They also functioned in community development, including road building, swamp drainage, and agricultural improvement. From the fifth century to the twelfth, the monasteries also provided both the vision and the manpower for effective missionary endeavor.[23]

Irish (Celtic) monasticism was especially prolific in providing missionaries. As a youth, the famous Patrick (died A.D. 461) was captured in his native southern Britain and taken to Ireland as a slave. At some point he had a spiritual conversion. After escaping and returning home, he had a vision imploring him to return to

[22]Bosch, *Transforming Mission*, 227.
[23]Ibid., 230.

Ireland. He subsequently returned and traveled widely, preaching an evangelical faith resulting in so many conversions that most of Ireland was considered Christian. The Irish Christians developed what was probably the most aggressive sense of mission of any church from the apostolic period to its time.

An early Irish monk, Columba (c. 521–597), established a monastery on the island of Iona, off the northwest shore of Britain. During the Viking era it was sacked at least twelve times, but for over two hundred years it poured out a stream of missionaries bent on Christianizing Europe. Although these Irish monks saw themselves as part of the universal Church, they at first operated independently of Rome, with significant differences in such issues as the date of Easter, and tonsure, for as yet the Roman church had not achieved ascendancy. Several other features of the monastic life in Ireland, including the design of their chapels, were clearly borrowed from Constantinople rather than from Rome. Later missionary expansion brought the Celtic and Roman efforts into increasing conflict until, finally, the Celtic missions had to yield to the authority of Rome. Their effect was great, especially among unreached peoples where they gained converts and prepared the way for future Christianization. In summary, Ralph Winter writes, "The Celts are the only nation in the first millennium who give an outstanding missionary response."[24]

Some have asked if the Irish monks' prime motivation for travel was not more the hope of achieving personal salvation than preaching salvation. To this, Bosch responds that pilgrimage was indeed a means of taking one's devotion to the extreme as the monk sought for spiritual perfection. This quest for perfection is attested to by a well-known eighth century Irish description of three levels of "martyrdom": white for the ascetic life,

---

[24]Winter, "Kingdom Strikes Back," B-5.

green for a higher level of contrition, and red for total self-mortification.[25] The monk was obliged to help those he met, so the goals of personal devotion and mission often merged.[26]

Benedict (A.D. 480–547) established the Benedictine monastic movement, noted for its "rule," which became the standard for Catholic monasticism and its missionary orientation. Gregory I (the Great) (540–604) was a Benedictine monk who first resisted becoming bishop of Rome and later shaped the papacy into the form that endured throughout the Middle Ages. Besides his administrative accomplishments, he is noted for his spiritual writings (commentaries and sermons) and for his missionary zeal.[27] He sent a group of forty missionaries to England in A.D. 596 under the leadership of Augustine, prior of St. Benedict's monastery in Rome.[28] Bosch considers this the first deliberate "foreign mission" in the sense in which this term was later used.[29]

Perhaps the most renowned of the medieval missionaries was Boniface, the apostle to Germany, "a man who had a deeper influence on the history of Europe than any Englishman who has ever lived."[30] Neill observes that Boniface began his missionary career at the age of forty, and his projects "were planned and calculated efforts on the part of mature men, based on a sober conviction that the Gospel of Christ must be preached to those who from their point of view were still barbarous peoples."[31] Boniface is specially noted for provoking a major "power encounter" when, in 724,

[25]Bosch, *Transforming Mission*, 231.
[26]Ibid., 233.
[27]Vos, *Exploring Church History*, 51–52.
[28]V. Raymond Edman, *The Light in Dark Ages* (Wheaton, Ill.: Van Kampen Press, 1949), 180.
[29]Bosch, *Transforming Mission*, 235.
[30]Neill, *Christian Missions*, 64 (quoting Christopher Dawson).
[31]Ibid., 64.

he cut down the sacred Oak of Thor, in the region of Hesse, for timber for a chapel. The Germans believed the gods would kill Boniface, but when he lived, they recognized that his God had power superior to that of Thor.[32]

In later medieval times, many monasteries became known for both their affluence and their corruption. Reforming movements sprang up, such as the one centered at Cluny (c. 910). These reforms came to be associated with such names as Bernard of Clairvaux, writer of such hymns as "Jesus, the Very Thought of Thee" and "O Sacred Head Now Wounded." Though some characterize all monasticism by its less noble examples, the medieval Roman Catholic model includes those that were mission oriented and spiritually attuned, such as those mentioned above.

Specific missionary orders that came with the development of monasticism should be noted by today's missionary movement. The Irish monks may have been seeking personal holiness, but they were nonetheless a group who removed themselves from the concerns of the wider church in order to focus upon a task that increasingly became overtly missionary. The same may be said of the Benedictine missionaries and members of the missionary orders of later centuries, such as the Friars and the Jesuits. These missionary orders greatly contributed to the expansion of the Roman Catholic Church both during the medieval period and after it. For now, let it be noted that the Church grew cross-culturally largely because of groups of dedicated individuals who were specifically set apart for a missionary purpose.

Conclusion

The medieval Roman Catholic missionary paradigm emphasized the growth of "Christendom." Gone were the days when evangelization was linked with the con-

---

[32]Ibid., 64–65.

stant expectation of the return of Christ. The Church had gone through tough times of political and philosophical challenge and emerged as a growing force to be reckoned with. The Christianity that spread was a Latinized version, emphasizing personal salvation that was believed to be found only within the established Church. The fusion of state and Church, begun with Constantine, manifested itself in sometimes dynamic and often oppressive regimes of mixed religious and political character. Though the individual must be saved, he did not have to understand, much less believe, Christian dogma; baptism would do the job, and various means of coercion were employed toward this objective. Oddly, within this rather negative setting there emerged a host of dedicated missionaries, martyrs, and godly monks.

The Church, though often misdirected and far from having a uniformly biblical faith, continued to grow. Although some of this growth was politically coerced, without a doubt there were significant centers of genuine spiritual enlightenment. Aberrant zeal within Christendom included the Crusades and the beginnings of colonialism. However misguided these may have been, they demonstrated a commitment by masses of people to their form of understanding of the Christian message.

As I have already noted, when the Church failed to reach out in missions, the unreached people of the frontier "reached in" to the homeland of the Church in military conquest. A similar pattern may be seen in the later medieval period, not in the conquest of the Christian base but in the fact that disaster followed misguided mission. The plague that killed more than one-third of Europe came after the debacle of the Crusades, the Church's misguided military campaigns against the Muslims. While cause-effect relation cannot be proven, the earlier observation that absence of mission invites military incursion might be amended to include the possibility that misguided mission may also be followed by some type of disaster. The principle is that those who receive the blessings of God (i.e., the gospel) must share them. Failure to share has been followed by calamity. Unlike the Irish national mission which brought blessing, there were three great missed opportunities when a strong Church failed to adequately propagate the faith beyond its borders: the peaceful interlude following Constantine, the strength and order within Europe at the zenith of the Holy Roman Empire, and the time of religious fervor associated with Cluniac reform and the Crusades. In each case, the absence of biblical mission was followed by disaster.[33]

STUDY QUESTIONS

1. What influence did the fusion of Church and state have upon the mission of the Church in medieval times?
2. The text refers to seven features of the medieval missions paradigm. Explain:
   a. What is meant by the changed context of the medieval Roman church.
   b. How Augustine contributed to an emphasis on "the individualization of salvation."
   c. Cyprian's view of salvation and how this concept in time redefined missions.
   d. The meaning of "mission between Church and state."
   e. The development of the concept of "indirect" and "direct" missionary wars.
   f. How "colonialism and mission" came to be the dominant missionary paradigm of the times.

---

[33]For further development of this thesis, including the possibility of a similar disaster upon today's church, see Winter, "Kingdom Strikes Back," B-16–21.

  g. The monastic missionary paradigm and how it contributed to the spread of Christianity.
3. Give examples of how those who had been neglected in evangelism became conquerors of lands thought to be "Christian." Comment on the concept that neglect of mission invites calamity.
4. Explain what the concept of "Christendom" came to mean within the time of the medieval period.

Chapter 9:

Shifting Paradigms

Period 3:
A.D. *1500–2000, Reformation, Enlightenment,*
Ecumenical, Evangelical, Pentecostal

"Protestant Reformation" is a term used to summarize the sixteenth century movement away from Roman Catholicism into newly recognized Protestant churches throughout Europe. Distinctives of the Reformation included the doctrines of justification by faith alone, salvation by grace alone, the Bible as the sole authority for doctrine and practice, the priesthood of the believer, and the promotion of congregational singing.[1]

The Reformation had many notable leaders, including Martin Luther, Huldrych Zwingli, and John Calvin. They emphasized, in addition to the above distinctives, correct preaching, correct observation of communion, and the rejection of the Catholic doctrines and practices that were viewed as unscriptural. Most of the energies of the Protestant churches went into the propagation of their distinctive views of the Bible's teaching on the issues of the day. Partly because of this preoccupation with these polemic issues, the cause of missions would not gain significant support until two hundred years had passed.

There were theological as well as practical reasons for this slow entry into missions. The theology of many

---

[1]Howard F. Vos, *Exploring Church History* (Nashville: Thomas Nelson, 1994), 87.

137

of the reformers stressed predestination. Some of their followers held that to preach to the heathen was to challenge God's predestinated order; others believed that the apostles had fulfilled the Great Commission. As knowledge of the world increased, the presence of higher religious ideals among pagan peoples led some to conclude that these peoples had once been evangelized but had rejected the gospel.

The Reformation produced churches that had broken with Rome, but it did not teach freedom of religion.[2] For example, the Holy Roman Empire recognized both Lutheranism and Roman Catholicism, but it required the people to follow the religion of their prince. Early in the Reformation, Catholic missions were sometimes respected as having validity and thus fulfilling any missionary obligation of the Protestant church. Many reformers believed the coming of Christ was imminent, but this belief did not motivate them to missions as it had the Early Church and would later do to those believing as the Early Church believed. Some try to defend the reformers on the basis that the entire Reformation was inherently missionary, biding its time for fuller expression; it seems better to acknowledge that for the most part the first leaders had other concerns and were simply silent on the subject of missions. As years passed and later generations of leaders were forced to address the subject of missions, they tended to defend the status quo and criticize those who advocated missions.[3] When the Protestants finally sent missionaries to Brazil and Lapland, it was in connection with colonial activity.

Renewed Missions Emphases

In contrast to the general position of the Reformation, the Pietists and Anabaptists represented a

---

[2]Ibid.
[3]David J. Bosch, *Transforming Mission: Paradigm Shifts in Theology of Mission* (Maryknoll, N.Y.: Orbis Books, 1991), 243–55.

strong missions commitment. They began as renewal movements within the state-recognized Reformed churches and only gradually moved toward autonomy. They considered church structure as going hand in hand with formalism, spiritual deadness, and lack of missionary zeal. Pietism stressed the new birth, sanctification, and warm religious experience. It clashed with the views of many reformers who said that the heathen were cursed, that if God wanted them saved He would accomplish this sovereignly, that there were no more apostles, and that the Great Commission had expired.[4]

Nikolaus von Zinzendorf (1700–60), founder of the Moravians, was among the leading Pietists of his time. His ideal was for volunteers from all walks of life to move in obedience to Christ and to the Holy Spirit, and to minister salvation and kindness to the spiritually and physically suffering. The Moravians responded in zealous commitment to this ideal. After a heavenly visitation in a prayer meeting, they determined that some should remain in prayer at all times. This prayer meeting continued without interruption for over one hundred years. When funds were not forthcoming to reach the mission fields of the West Indies, would-be missionaries sold themselves as indentured servants to work in the sugar plantations and preach Christ among the workers there. John Wesley visited their center and, largely through their influence, came to have the assurance of eternal life that launched his ministry as the founder of Methodism and preacher of salvation whose parish was the world.

Three aspects of the Moravian approach to missions should be noted. The first is that they believed God was sending them, so they did not view their service as an assigned duty of the Church. In this they differed from their times. Where missions existed at all, the concept was that of individuals sent by state churches to serve

---

[4]Ibid., 253.

under their own flag on foreign soil; church and state were thus closely linked (as they had been in one way or another since Constantine). In breaking with this model, the Moravians were setting a precedent that has influenced missions to this day. They were also in direct conflict with church, state, and colonial authorities.

However, it is important to see that the Moravians' emphasis on being sent by God anticipated the modern missiological concept *missio Dei* (mission of God),[5] missionaries being sent in response to divine initiative, God's mission in which humankind participates. Of course, placing this present understanding on the eighteenth century Moravians would be anachronous.

The second noteworthy aspect of Moravian missions is the concept that missions should be undertaken by the common people of the church. The Roman Catholic precedent had been mission undertaken largely by monks. Although many were skilled in trades, they all functioned as religious professionals. By contrast, the Moravians were anything but religious professionals. They had typically never undergone any religious orders or the discipline of theological study. Rather, they were lay people with burning hearts willing to pay their own expenses for the opportunity to bear witness to the unreached, both at home and abroad.

A third significant aspect of Moravian missions was that they solved the problem of manpower. As it had for centuries, the monastery functioned as a source of seemingly limitless manpower for missions. The Roman Catholic Church almost always had replacements for those who were martyred. New fields had seldom lacked for those who would plant the cross. The Protestants, by contrast, had little vision for missions and no plan to reproduce missions personnel. Among all the reasons commonly given for the Reformed churches' delayed entry into missions, this is

---

[5]Ibid., 257.

the one that is sometimes overlooked: The reformers had discarded the monastery without devising an alternative means of recruiting workers. The Moravians, with their extended prayer meetings, warm feelings from the Holy Spirit, and groaning and tears for the lost, were able, without conscious effort, to replicate the Catholic's ability to field a missionary team. Although Catholic missionary orders dwarfed Moravian numbers, the Moravians moved expeditiously to the fields of their calling and in so doing, provided a model effective even to the present.

Besides Pietism, other renewal movements within the Reformed tradition occurred in the seventeenth century. Puritanism was one such renewal. The Puritans actively promoted missions among the colonies of the New World. Puritan John Eliot, "Apostle to the Indians," labored for fifty years among the Native Americans of Massachusetts. It is significant that this missions vision was supervised by the New England Company and the Society for the Propagation of the Gospel in New England, among the first Protestant missionary societies.[6] Puritanism within colonial America incorporated a strong social concern. Puritan eschatology taught that Jews and Gentiles would join in the true Church in a final period of great expansion. They fully believed this expansion would come in the last days that had then begun. In short, they fully expected remarkable results in both conversions and subsequent elevation of living conditions. It is interesting that their fervent commitment to this eschatological understanding seems to have contributed greatly to the success they expected.

In time, the European Reformed churches began to

---

[6]Ibid. See also Charles L. Chaney, *The Birth of Missions in America* (Pasadena: William Carey Library, 1976), 106–7; R. Pierce Beaver, *Pioneers in Mission: Early Missionary Ordination Sermons, Charges, and Instructions* (Grand Rapids: Wm. B. Eerdmans, 1966), 2–6.

awaken to missions. This came about, at least in part, through the influence of Pietistic groups such as the Moravians and the missions societies that began to spring up after William Carey went to India in 1793. Carey was a shoemaker who also taught school and pastored a small group of nonconformists. He had been influenced by the Moravians, greatly admiring their missionary purpose. He became convinced that the Great Commission was still in effect and that God expected Christians to "use means" to bring about the conversion of the heathen. Though at first rebuffed, he was later successful in bringing together a group who founded the Baptist Missionary Society. Carey promptly volunteered to go overseas, and he and a colleague were the first to be sent.

Carey was successful in accomplishing at least three major objectives that influenced all subsequent evangelical missions history. First, he was able to write an effective Scriptural rationale for missions, with the result that public opinion changed, first in Britain and then throughout Europe. Second, he and his colleagues devised the means of forming a society completely dedicated to missionary work. The idea of mission societies was thus born (and as a consequence, the Baptist Missionary Society). Third, he addressed the problem of manpower by himself volunteering to go. In this way, the precedent was set that those who felt the call would offer their services to a missions board, resign their appointments or positions in their home land, and relocate to another country with the express purpose of opening what today would be called evangelical churches.

Although heavily influenced by Moravian thought, the Baptist Missionary Society was different in several respects. It was not connected to any state church, not even to a revival movement within such a church. Whereas the early Moravians wanted to preach the gospel without starting churches, Carey, along with

Joshua Marshman and William Ward (the Serampore [India] Trio), set out to do just that—and succeeded in starting more than twenty-six within Carey's lifetime. They also translated the Scriptures into many languages and dialects and established a major printing enterprise. Without seemingly neglecting any other duties, Carey accepted heavy responsibility for teaching Indian languages within a newly formed college. For many years he commuted several miles by boat each week to develop this academic program and train its students. He was also a passionate student of natural history and in his early career earned his living as foreman of an indigo plant, all while pursuing an incredible schedule of translation and evangelization.

What Carey bequeathed to his and succeeding generations was the assurance that once God's will became known through patient study of the Scriptures, believers were responsible to find appropriate means to accomplish that will. The particular means Carey and his colleagues devised became the basic template followed by most evangelical missions to this day. That template was the setting up of a missions society, the sending out of qualified volunteers to become church planters, and the widening of their vision to accomplish a wide variety of activities consistent with their primary objective. Later "faith missions," such as Hudson Taylor's China Inland Mission (founded 1865), following that template, came into being specifically to reach the vast interiors of lands where the gospel had made little penetration beyond the coastal cities.

The Effects of Rationalism

The eighteenth century marked the coming-of-age of rationalism. Three men did much to prepare the way. Copernicus (1473–1543) taught that the sun, not the earth, was the center the planets revolved around. Descartes (1596–1650) taught that the universe ran according to mathematical equation. Francis Bacon

(1561–1626) stressed the inductive method of learning.

The mood of the times became one of questioning centuries-old suppositions. Governments were now held to be in social contract with the people they governed. Those governments that failed to provide for their subjects were to be replaced. Theology, with its centuries of imbibing the superstitions of the half-converted, found itself the recipient of a great deal of hostility. In many cases, theologians responded by illogical syncretism. Absurd claims were defended on the basis that they were "Christian." Rationalists attacked the Reformed churches although the Reformed doctrine of *sola scriptura* had long since eliminated a good deal of what Rationalists objected to. Still, as Christians meeting in churches, Reformed and Pietistic groups were suspect among the alienated and educated.

Groups such as the Moravians and the Methodists, with their emphasis upon personal conversion, continued to fare well. In effect, they served to stem the hemorrhaging of Christendom in their time. Still, a new worldview was coming into effect, that of the Enlightenment.

The Enlightenment believed that science could explain all the mysteries formerly attributed to God. Following the writings of the intellectuals of their own and recent centuries, Enlightenment writers reinterpreted historical records, folk tales, and contemporary supernatural perceptions. To Enlightenment writers, the biblical accounts of miracles were simply the efforts of a prescientific age to explain natural phenomena. They considered Jesus only a noble example and perhaps the greatest teacher who ever lived, but not the divine Son of God. Eschatology, if believed at all, was this-worldly and was to be accomplished through human means. They considered churches a bit behind the times and irrelevant. They looked at the Bible as a product of endless redaction. They called the history of Israel an epic tale devised by well-intentioned priests who recognized the need for a cultus around which people must rally in order to survive. Therefore, biblical miracles were considered nonscientific; biblical history, nonhistoric; and biblical prophecy, irrelevant.

The Enlightenment mindset gradually changed the approach of the Church to missions. Many churches found that their clergy no longer believed in the lostness of humankind. Christ's teaching that " 'I am the way' " (John 14:26) and the subsequent statement in Acts that there is " 'no other name' " (Acts 4:12) were both embarrassments. These clergy still felt that they were Christian and greatly wanted to do missions. However, the focus of their missions throughout the nineteenth century became the application of modern technical capability to solve the social problems of life.

These processes continued into the early twentieth-century; then evangelical (i.e. "fundamentalist") backlash arose. They limited their mission to the spiritual by identifying any social concern with the liberal agenda. Those living at the turn of that century may not have recognized it, but the Enlightenment had changed a widely held missionary paradigm. For those who came to be called liberals, the Enlightenment had provided a scientific mindset in which they continued to minister to the hurting of the world. For those of evangelical faith, the Enlightenment was bringing an end to an era of public consensus that Christian missions was a noble venture. Now, Christian missions that aimed at conversion to Christ began to be suspect as culturally insensitive, bigoted, arrogant, and intolerant. It is significant that the Student Volunteer Movement peaked in 1910 when thousands attended its Edinburgh conference, but had ceased to have any meaningful function by the early 1930s. Evangelical Christians who wished to be missionaries could no longer expect the unqualified commendation of the "Christian cultures" they had come from.

An evangelical shunning of social concern was not as

thoroughgoing as some have imagined.[7] Taken as a group, Evangelical Christians have always demonstrated a strong sense of social conscience and concern. Many who felt their groups had been frightened to some degree from social concern have come to believe evangelicals should be leaders in the fields of compassionate and social concern. While there are many different postures relating to evangelical social concern, evangelicals seem to have generally defended their evangelistic (i.e., Great Commission) orientation from their critics while at the same time reasserting the evangelical presence on the field of compassion.

As the twentieth century closed, there were many indicators that the Enlightenment had oversold its potential and was losing sway over most Western societies.[8] In one sense, an extreme social development of the Enlightenment was expressed in Marxism, a structured social order in which scientific advance promised equality for all, an order in which religion was not needed. The demise of this system within much of the world testifies to its inability to speak to the needs of modern humanity.

Neoorthodoxy

A theological movement beginning in the early twentieth century and known as neoorthodoxy represented another testimonial to the inadequacy of the Enlightenment. Enlightenment writers had anticipated the demise of religion. Instead, religion continued to flourish all over the world.[9] Human beings are, indeed, religious beings. At the risk of oversimplifying complex issues, neoorthodoxy may be seen as an attempt to

---

[7]The National Association of Evangelicals, for example, has always been active in meeting needs of the unfortunate.
[8]Bosch, *Transforming Mission;* see the entire discussion, 262–367.
[9]Classical liberalism (e.g., Friedrich Schleiermacher, 1768–1834) did recognize this.

recover a dynamic spiritual dimension for those whose faith had been wounded in their passage through the educational processes of the Enlightenment.[10]

All this has enormous ramifications for those engaged in Christian mission. First, it has long been recognized that missions workers coming from societies that embraced the Enlightenment paradigm sometimes experience difficulty while ministering among more traditional societies. Western missionaries who lack a supernatural approach to life have little credibility in much of the world.

Second, those who would minister the gospel in societies that have been influenced by the Enlightenment as it is losing its grasp should be aware that the questions they will face may be, in effect, post-Enlightenment. The vacuum left by two centuries of the Enlightenment will be replaced by something. If the Creator of heaven and earth is not presented as the answer to the world's need, pseudo-gods in abundance will come calling. In short, the Enlightenment stripped much of the world of its credulity in matters of faith. Yet, human beings long for God. There has never been a more opportune moment to present " 'the way and the truth and the life' " (John 14:6) to the masses of humanity.

Third, although many evangelicals have returned to their historical confession of faith,[11] today's Pentecostal Christians stand at the forefront of mission to the post-Enlightenment world. Pentecostals have retained their belief in the miracle-working God of the Bible, they are able to preach the Bible with authority, and their testimonies ring true.

---

[10]For example, Karl Barth's move in the direction of neoorthodoxy marked his rejection of the classical liberalism of his teacher, Adolf von Harnack.

[11]Ultradispensationalists among them deny that miracles and gifts of the Spirit are for today. However, dispensational theology by its renewed emphasis on the imminent return of Christ did motivate missions.

The Ecumenical Movement

The ecumenical movement believes it represents Christ's desire for unity among His followers (John 17:21—22). Many observers have felt that the modern ecumenical movement was Christianity's best hope for a united representation of Christ to a divided world.[12]

Evangelicals, however, have often expressed serious reservations about this movement. First, they find it difficult to make common cause with groups that include high-profile individuals whose public statements diverge from the historic Christian faith. Evangelicals do not wish to be labeled judgmental, but they often feel their mission is different from that of groups that seem to deny the validity of the Scriptures and the Christian experience based upon them.

Second, the ecumenical movement is often seen as blunting the evangelistic agenda. "Conversion" has become a bad word to many members within a pluralistic society. Liberals among them hold that all religions are valid expressions of truth. Repentance, new birth, regeneration, and the infilling of the Holy Spirit are foreign concepts. Some within the ecumenical movement appear to advocate religious pluralism and a narrow tolerance, critical of those who take literally Jesus Christ's exclusive truth claims.

Pentecostal Missions

We will now turn to the consideration of the Pentecostal paradigm. Pentecostals see the outpouring of the Holy Spirit worldwide upon true believers in Christ as heralding a final era of harvest. Missions is far from going out of date. In fact, missions is just gaining momentum among many of the newer churches in this final age, the age of the Spirit. Although Pentecostals have a great deal in common with other evangelicals,

---

[12]Bosch, *Transforming Mission*, 368–510.

the Pentecostal movement has its own distinctive missions paradigm. As with each paradigm that has been considered, missions practice is complex, and there are many exceptions to the major features of the Pentecostal's paradigm. I would suggest, however, that the following are typical.

Pentecostals believe that the Holy Spirit has been poured out upon the Church as an enduement of power to accomplish the discipling of the nations. This belief is based upon the teachings of Christ and the apostles, especially in such texts as Acts 1:8, in which Christ stated that the purpose of the infilling of the Holy Spirit would be to bear witness of Him to the ends of the earth. Pentecostals encourage believers to be filled with the Holy Spirit so that the Church may evangelize the world before Christ's return. As Everett A. Wilson writes in *Strategy of the Spirit,* "The Assemblies of God emphasized, as did other Pentecostals, the indispensability of the individual's crisis experience as the energizing force of the Christian faith and the coordinating principle of the church."[13]

Several ramifications of the Pentecostal position should be recognized. First, the Pentecostal movement's orientation is primarily Christological. Pentecostals believe the power of the Holy Spirit is given to preach Christ. They believe in His virgin birth, sinless life, miracles, death, resurrection, and personal return. The validity of supposed supernatural experiences or revival phenomena is judged by the resulting power to preach Christ in such a way that conviction of sin takes place, lives are changed, and the Church grows. Religious experience is rejected if it does not lift Christ up or if it runs counter to the biblical record.

Second, Pentecostal experience results in the conviction of sin. In John 16:8–11 Jesus promised that when

---

[13]Everett A. Wilson, *Strategy of the Spirit* (London: Paternoster, Regnum Books, 1997), 4.

the Holy Spirit came He would convict the world of sin, righteousness, and judgment. Pentecostals believe that they are filled with the Holy Spirit in order to minister that sense of conviction to the world, without which it will not come to Christ for salvation. Even though Pentecostal churches are often among the leaders in promoting responsible church-growth methodologies, the consensus of the movement has never been that these methodologies are the primary cause of church growth. Rather, Pentecostals believe their churches grow because they are Pentecostal. When churches do not grow, the Pentecostal approach to this problem is more often spiritual than methodological: Believers fast, pray, and reach out to the lost and hurting within their environment until something changes.[14]

Third, the Pentecostal paradigm of missions has also historically included a strong identification with the poor, suffering, and marginalized of society. Whether in Western or non-Western countries, Pentecostals have reached out to the hurting and suffering both spontaneously and by design. Douglas Petersen's *Not By Might, Nor By Power* has described the contribution of this orientation to the growth of the church in Central America.[15] Pentecostals, always eager to help in times of natural disaster and war, have recently taken steps to systematize and enlarge their approach to compassionate ministries in view of the magnitude of modern disasters.

Pentecostals have always been people of the miraculous. The Enlightenment challenged the validity of the

---

[14]For a further treatment of elenctics (conviction) see David J. Hesselgrave, *Communicating Christ Cross-Culturally*, 2d. ed. (Grand Rapids: Zondervan Publishing House, 1991), 581–86, 610–11, 638.
[15]Douglas Petersen, *Not By Might Nor By Power* (Irvine, Calif.: Paternoster, Regnum Books, 1996); see also Gary B. McGee, *This Gospel Shall Be Preached*, vol. 1 (Springfield, Mo.: Gospel Publishing House, 1986); and Wilson, *Strategy of the Spirit.*

supernatural; reports of the miraculous, whether within the biblical record, church history, or the contemporary church, were all viewed as explainable by natural law. Pentecostals have always taken exception to this Enlightenment worldview. Such exception is not unique to Pentecostals; however, evangelicals who accept the miraculous in biblical times may also reject the miraculous in postapostolic times, including the modern era. Their view of dispensations has led some to such a position. Pentecostals would see this position as due to the Enlightenment.[16] The validity of miracles was not generally challenged between the time of the apostles and the time of the Enlightenment. Some early believers did indeed reject spiritual gifts, especially prophecy (e.g., those who opposed the Montanists), but they did not typically reject miracles in general. Pentecostals see their own movement as a corrective: restoring to the Church the sense of the supernatural stolen by the Enlightenment.[17]

Pentecostals expect growth. (Harvest-related themes and metaphors abound throughout the history of Pentecostalism's popular theology.) And with growth they expect to serve. Since the Lord has given the spiritual enablement needed to evangelize the world (Acts 1:8), Pentecostals fully expect the Church to succeed in this task. They see the power of the Holy Spirit not as a denominational distinctive but as a blessing available to all true believers as a means for accomplishing the harvest. They further expect the Holy Spirit to enable them to minister to the needs of the hurting while bringing the gospel to all the nations.

---

[16]Many nondispensational evangelicals also reject miracles and the gifts of the Spirit for today for other reasons; e.g., B. B. Warfield, *Counterfeit Miracles* (London: Banner of Truth Trust, 1918).

[17]For an in-depth presentation of this view, see Paul A. Pomerville, *The Third Force in Missions* (Peabody, Mass.: Hendrickson Publishers, 1985).

Fourth, another feature of the Pentecostal missions paradigm is its emphasis upon God's inclusiveness in the accomplishment of the harvest.[18] For example, the Pentecostal movement is heavily indebted to women for the understanding and accomplishment of its vision. Since women are baptized in the Holy Spirit and receive the various *charismata,* Pentecostals throughout the world recognize and appreciate their service. This is true even among those Pentecostals who do not formally credential women as ministers. Thus, opponents attempting to discredit the Pentecostal movement have disparagingly referred to it as a "women's movement." Both men and women, however, have given time, energy, and finances to visit other lands in order to evangelize, build churches, and otherwise aid missionaries. This is a tremendous manifestation of the universal priesthood of believers.

All races and social classes are likewise attracted to the Pentecostal movement. The fact that Pentecostal churches have often reached the underprivileged has not kept them from appealing as well to the elite of society.[19]

Yet another feature of the Pentecostal missions paradigm has been its emphasis upon the centrality of the Bible as the written Word of God. A hallmark of Pentecostal believers worldwide has been their commitment to Bible reading, Scripture memorization, and respect for the authority of God's Word. They are heirs of *sola scriptura.* For many years, Pentecostals have stated without fear of contradiction that they have more Bible schools for ministerial training than their non-Pentecostal evangelical counterparts. There have always been notable Bible scholars among Pentecostals,

---

[18]In this, Pentecostals are true heirs of the Reformation reemphasis upon the universal priesthood of believers.

[19]A number of early Pentecostal leaders, such as Elmer Fisher and J. Narver Gortner, were college and seminary graduates.

and their number has been steadily increasing in recent decades. However, Pentecostals are noted most for their widespread practical training of pastors and laity.

Pentecostal Missiology

This emphasis upon Pentecostal distinctives as the movement's key to growth does not mean that the movement is without a distinctive missiology. The two concepts that have most widely defined Pentecostal missiology are those of *the indigenous church* and *partnership.*

THE CONCEPT OF THE INDIGENOUS CHURCH

"Indigenous church" as a concept among Pentecostals includes the same three elements that identify it for others, namely self-government, self-propagation, and self-support. The concept was developed and popularized by Rufus Anderson (1796–1880) of the American Board of Commissioners for Foreign Missions and Henry Venn (1796–1873) of the Church Missionary Society in London.[20] Alice E. Luce, an early proponent of the "three selfs" within the Assemblies of God, wrote a three-part series on the indigenous church for the *Pentecostal Evangel* in early 1921.[21] However, within Pentecostal circles the best known exponent of its principles was Melvin L. Hodges, professor, field secretary, and missionary within the Assemblies of God. Since, in recent years, the "three-selfs" model has had its critics (most of whom agree with the major part of the model), it is important to capture the essence of these three elements as they have functioned within the Pentecostal approach to missions.[22]

---

[20]Gary B. McGee, *This Gospel Shall Be Preached,* 1:30.
[21]Ibid., 97.
[22]Melvin L. Hodges's best known book, *The Indigenous Church* (Springfield, Mo.: Gospel Publishing House, 1976), was first published in 1953. It was picked up and published by Moody Press as well. It is still used as a textbook in some places.

Hodges always began with the element of self-government, because he regarded it as the controlling dynamic of all three selfs. He taught that local churches did not require foreign missionaries as pastors, for local people everywhere are fully capable of preaching and teaching the word of God and administering their own affairs. In fact, he warned that a church accustomed to a foreign missionary as pastor might come to reject a local pastor. He further advised that local people should decide on who would be admitted to church membership and that discipline must come from the local people themselves to be effective.

Interestingly, Hodges' chapter on self-government makes no mention of the government of a national organization. When he does come to this topic later in his book, he advises delay in setting up such an organization until the number of churches have sufficiently multiplied so that the presence of missionaries will not overwhelm national church leaders. Even so, he recognizes that foreign missionaries may well hold some positions within the national church structure, provided they do so respectfully and recognize the proper time for transition.[23]

Some friendly critics have supposed that "self-government" implied something of a xenophobic exclusion of foreigners, especially missionaries, from church leadership on all levels.[24] Pentecostals have taken their cue from writers such as Hodges. Their idea of self-government is simply the recognition, locally and nationally, that God has gifted the local people the same as He has anyone else, so they may be trusted under God to accomplish His will.

---

[23]Hodges, *Indigenous Church*, 22–41, 92–97.

[24]For an example of a friendly critic of the "indigenous church" whose criticism shows that he has defined the three "selfs" differently from Hodges, see William A. Smalley, "Cultural Implications of an Indigenous Church," in *Perspectives on the World Christian Movement*, ed. Ralph D. Winter and Steven C. Hawthorne, rev. ed. (Pasadena: William Carey Library, 1992), C-149–157.

Hodges treated self-propagation next. The basic building block of self-propagation is spontaneous lay witness. New believers, if truly regenerated, typically have a strong desire to share their faith with friends and relatives, and they should by all means be encouraged to do so. As a church fills with people, it should do on the corporate level what the believers have done on the individual level—that is, share its faith, in this case by opening extensions. These extensions will in turn grow, being nurtured in the faith by an extension worker who becomes a lay pastor. This process repeats itself until the whole countryside is filled with churches.

Hodges saw the role of the missionary in the beginning to be that of an evangelist, bringing the gospel to a new field. As people believe and churches are established, the missionary travels in a circuit, visiting each station periodically to check the progress of the local believers. He takes lay workers with him as he travels, so as to share the vision for the region with these "Timothys." The presence of such coworkers also trains the new churches to see nonforeign workers as equally gifted and capable of spiritual ministry. The missionary naturally has moved to his next role, that of teacher, training co-workers and launching them into ministry.

The Pentecostal paradigm also recognizes salvation-healing crusades as an essential part of the plan. The masses, especially in the cities, will not be reached without some means of attracting their attention to the person of Jesus. Hodges emphasizes this type of evangelism under his unit on self-propagation on the basis that Jesus and the apostles are the biblical model; they brought miraculous healing to the sick as they taught the kingdom of God. Pentecostals have not missed the point. If they would pattern their ministries after Jesus and the apostles, they must preach salvation and expect the Lord to confirm the Word with signs following. And this is exactly what He does, providing a major key of self-propagation. As people witness the sick being healed, they recognize the churches as centers of supernatural power, and they grow accordingly.

As an adjunct to self-propagation, Hodges wrote about training leadership. His appeal was to train toward the objective, not away from it: He warned against training only bright young men and forgetting the more mature, natural leaders whom the people would follow. He stressed training the entire church. He pointed out how missionaries were often responsible for leaders that do not lead, for they have at times designed systems that do not encourage initiative or that do not feel right to the local people. He especially warned against the danger of missionaries setting up any form of training that has a life of its own outside the church, rather than functioning as a ministry of the church.

Although most Pentecostals would agree on the basic model for self-propagation as set forth by Hodges, to achieve the ideal sometimes proves difficult. Nevertheless, those Pentecostal churches that operate as Hodges suggested generally have experienced a strong level of self-propagation.

Though self-support is sometimes seen as almost the whole indigenous church paradigm, Hodges placed it third as the most reasonable means of accomplishing the first two objectives. At stake is a major issue: Are people from economically depressed regions able to tithe and support their pastors and local churches? Most Pentecostals, along with Hodges, would answer affirmatively both on the basis of Scripture and on the basis of Pentecostal experience. The Scriptural pattern of the Old Testament was clearly based upon the system of tithing, and none were considered too poor to participate. Within the New Testament, it would appear that the people willingly gave far more than a tithe. In 2 Corinthians 8:2–3, Paul commended the Macedonian churches (i.e., Philippi) for their "rich generosity" in giving "beyond their ability." In Philippians 4:10–19, he thanked and praised these churches for their generosity.

Especially significant, in view of their poverty, was the benediction of verse 19: "And my God will meet all your needs according to his glorious riches in Christ Jesus." Within the Pentecostal paradigm for missions, these verses are taken seriously, and even the poorest believers are urged to tithe and give beyond the tithe. Since God has given these believers the gift of salvation, the baptism in the Holy Spirit, and attendant spiritual gifts and graces, it is not difficult for them to believe that their material needs are of concern to God and will be met by His abundant provision. That this indeed happens is the Pentecostal testimony in country after country.

Some have supposed that self-support implies economic isolation. The gift Paul carried to the Jerusalem church has been cited as an illustration of self-support having its limits, since that gift may be regarded as outside assistance for a church that should have been self-supporting.[25] Self-support, however, as taught by Hodges and understood by Pentecostals deals with a much more basic issue: Can a local body of believers anywhere in the world assume financial responsibility for itself? Can the gospel become indigenous in every culture, or are some cultures so economically deprived that the gospel must remain identified as foreign because local expenses must continually be met with outside funding? Hodges's contention that the churches of any country should be self-supporting has been generally accepted and should be regarded as a basic component of the Pentecostal paradigm. The issues of disaster relief or assistance with major national or international projects are certainly complex issues that must be carefully resolved, but they represent something of a graduate course, beyond the immediate scope of the appeal for self-support.[26]

---

[25]Ibid., C-150.
[26]The Assemblies of God Division of Foreign Missions has a definite humanitarian relief emphasis.

Among Hodges' major points that would be generally supported by Pentecostal churches are the following:[27]

- All churches should give, because it is biblical.
- Churches need to give to be spiritually strong.
- Local churches will be regarded as foreign and will not be respected if they are foreign-funded.
- Foreign funding limits church growth, because explosive church growth typically occurs as a result of local excitement including giving to accomplish objectives that the local people believe in.
- Foreign support of pastors leads to their being emotionally tied to the foreign mission rather than to the church they pastor.
- Local churches and pastors will be better off financially in the long term if they are locally funded.

THE CONCEPT OF PARTNERSHIP

Next to the indigenous church concept, the concept of partnership may be regarded as the strongest organizational component of the Pentecostal paradigm of missions. An Assemblies of God contemporary of Melvin Hodges, Morris Williams, wrote what is usually regarded as the definitive work on this subject.[28] The book, *Partnership*, is dedicated to the concept that especially in missions no one can say to another, "I have no need of you." Rather, for the Great Commission to be fulfilled, dynamic international partnerships must develop. This will result in a team approach to missions.

Throughout Williams's lifetime, the major question was the relationship between the missionary fellowships of the sending mission and the national organizations of indigenous churches. Rather than their

---

[27]Hodges, *Indigenous Church*, 74–91.
[28]Morris Williams, *Partnership in Mission* (Springfield, Mo.: Assemblies of God Division of Foreign Missions, 1979).

maturing into isolation, Williams proposed an ideal illustrated by two overlapping circles. Each circle should be respected as having its own identity, but the two should operate in partnership, as shown by the overlapping areas. During the first phase, the pioneering phase, the area of overlap was much larger. What the model accomplished for mission and church was the mutual understanding of how "phase two" might function. This pattern has been widely followed by Pentecostal churches with the result that national churches have valued the foreign presence and investment without the compromise of their essential autonomy. For the sending mission, the key to the success of partnership rests upon two major understandings. The first is that the terms of the partnership must be understood as undergoing continual reevaluation. The missionary has no permanent sphere. An annual partnership meeting is recommended as a time of reevaluation. The second key to success is to recognize that partnership rests upon a foundation of mutual respect and warm personal relationships. There must be ongoing love, prayer, and fellowship. In short, unless genuine and abiding friendship develops between the partners, their relationship cannot hope to achieve the goals for which it was formed.

The current mission statement of the Division of Foreign Missions of the USA Assemblies of God shows most of the components of the Pentecostal paradigm of missions implicitly or explicitly:

> Our mission: REACHING. We are proclaiming the message of Jesus Christ to the spiritually lost in all the world through every available means. PLANTING. We are establishing churches in more than 150 nations, following the New Testament pattern. TRAINING. We are training leaders throughout the world to proclaim the message of Jesus Christ to their own people and to other nations. TOUCHING. We are touching poor and suffering people with the compassion of Jesus Christ and inviting them to become His followers.[29]

---

[29]*Pentecostal Evangel*, 8 December 1998, 1.

Explicit statements include proclamation, the centrality of Jesus Christ, the priority of church planting, the priority of missions-focused leadership training, and compassionate concern within the overall context of inviting the world to come to Christ. Implicit in the New Testament pattern is the Pentecostal understanding of the dynamic atmosphere in which reaching, planting, training, and touching are to take place. Also implicit is the understanding that "the New Testament pattern" includes the Pentecostal practices of the New Testament Church, the apocalyptic worldview of that Church, and the indigenous aspects of the New Testament pattern of church planting. The training plank clearly implies the priority that is placed upon what is sometimes called "training beyond the indigenous church." That is, the mission objectives of "the Church" should be the mission objectives of the Church in each nation of the world. Stated differently, there should be a full participation of the former "mission field" in the task of world missions until Jesus returns. Finally, the compassion statement reflects the historic understanding of the biblical mandate in this area. Without implying that compassion is not worthy within its own right, the statement clearly sees compassion (as with everything else the Church does) as an announcement of the good news that Jesus is Lord. In fact, there is increasing emphasis on compassionate ministries.

Summary

In summary, the first period of missions until A.D. 500 was marked by an apostolic commitment to missions before Christ's return. The Church saw this as its assigned task. When the Church was outreach-oriented with an apocalyptic and pneumatological mindset, it experienced rapid growth both spontaneously and by design. As the Church became Hellenized, it became more able to defend itself within the world of its times but suffered the inevitable encroachments of that world.

The second period of missions, 500 to 1500, was designated as the medieval Roman Catholic period. When the Church grew for societal rather than spiritual reasons, joined hands with the state, and became highly organized, it lost its apocalyptic orientation to mission, replacing this earlier passion with the concept of "extending Christendom." While this period is marked by notable saintly personages and heroic missionary accomplishment, the overall direction of the Church was toward that spiritual morass often referred to as the Dark Ages. Mission took on the means of direct and indirect missionary wars that finally led to the debacle of the Crusades. Christianity was thus associated with the political realm to such a degree that the emergence of colonialism would be viewed by many as synonymous with mission.

The third period, 1500 to the present, has been marked by the paradigms of Reformation, Enlightenment, the Ecumenical Movement, Evangelicalism, and Pentecostalism. When the Protestant Reformers stressed justification by faith without stressing mission, many of them in effect yielded missions to the Catholic Church. When the Enlightenment posed an increasing challenge to historic faith, pietistic renewal emerged in such groups as the Moravians, providing both a missions reorientation to the church and an experience-oriented reply to the Enlightenment.[30] During these times, pioneers such as William Carey and Hudson Taylor championed the cause of fulfilling the Great Commission through devising means to reach the lost, even the lost in the great interior regions of the world. From this fire, modern evangelicalism has lit its lamp of mission.

---

[30]Unfortunately, this experience-oriented approach also produced classical liberalism, such as that of Schleiermacher (1768–1834).

With the modernist-fundamentalist controversy, some evangelicals retreated from ministries of compassion, which had become associated with modernism. Most have since recovered an involvement in compassionate ministries within the context of their Great Commission orientation. When Pentecostalism became a major missions force, it contributed to the wider church a renewed sense of spiritual power. This power demonstrated God's intention to accomplish His will through His covenant people in view of Christ's return.

Conclusion

There have been three major turning points in modern missions. The first is identified with William Carey. The Protestant Reformation achieved spiritual reform—but not in the field of mission. It was left to William Carey to challenge the geographical limitations placed upon the gospel by the historic church-state fusion. He planted the seeds for the Church's growth beyond Europe.

The second turning point deals with the post-Enlightenment mission of the Church. When the Enlightenment swept away superstition and then assumed the scientific method could demythologize the supernatural, the pietistic renewal answered with primarily a demonstration of mission. As God had done in the past, He did in the present: moved supernaturally. Pentecostalism has continued this response, especially through its contribution in the field of Lukan pneumatology.[31] Pentecostals have demonstrated that

---

[31]See, for example, Roger Stronstad, "The Hermeneutics of Lucan Historiography," *Paraclete* 22 (fall 1988): 6–11; Robert P. Menzies, "The Distinctive Character of Luke's Pneumatology," *Paraclete* 25 (fall 1991): 18. See also Stronstad's books *The Charismatic Theology of St. Luke* (Peabody, Mass.: Hendrickson Publishers, 1984); and *Spirit, Scripture, and Theology: A Pentecostal Perspective* (Baguio City, Philippines: Asia Pacific Theological Seminary Press, 1995).

the primitive faith viewed God's miraculous intervention as normative within the context of mission. The supernatural is thus normal and necessary if the Church is to participate in fulfilling *missio Dei*. Now, with the decline of the Enlightenment as a dominant social paradigm, the Church at large seems to show great acceptance of the supernatural role of the Holy Spirit within the context of mission.

The third turning point is one now in process. Many believers within the Pentecostal-charismatic tradition have come to see that experience-oriented religion becomes self-centered. The present emphasis upon the biblical theology of missions comes as an answer to this problem. Pentecostal experience without a commitment to fulfill the mission of God will lead to excess. As Carey once rescued the Church from its European containment, it is now time for the Church to move from present forms of isolation. The Church cannot afford to be encapsulated in a celebration of blessing. A Pentecostal paradigm of missions, anchored in a biblical theology of missions, thus stands as today's "means" to accomplish the mission of the Church. It looks to the future success of God's stated mission revealed throughout Scripture, culminating in a Spirit-filled Church expecting Christ's imminent return as it makes disciples from among all nations.

STUDY QUESTIONS

1. Since the Reformation stressed a return to the Scriptures, why did it take about two hundred years for missions to come into favor within the Reformed church?
2. Explain three significant contributions made by the Moravians to the modern missionary movement.
3. How did the New England Puritans' view of eschatology contribute to their view of the mission of the Church?

4. Describe the significance of William Carey's three major contributions to the evangelical understanding of missions.

5. In what ways did the Enlightenment change popular thinking with respect to the mission of the Church?

6. The Enlightenment paradigm has influenced Christian thought and at times occasioned backlash. Describe the influence or relationship of the Enlightenment on conservative evangelicals in the early twentieth century, neoorthodoxy, and the ecumenical movement.

7. Explain the ecumenical paradigm of mission.

8. Describe the most characteristic features of the Pentecostal paradigm of missions.

9. Describe the essential features of Melvin Hodges's approach to the indigenous church.

10. Describe the essential features of Morris Williams's approach to partnership.

11. In your own words, describe some of the major paradigms of missions history in terms of a "when/then" construction.

12. Three major turning points are given in modern missions. Evaluate each of these.

UNIT 3:
THE CHALLENGE OF THE FUTURE

Those concerned with missions expansion and development often focus on the frontiers of geography, ethnicity, and society. These frontiers may be effectively reached, however, only by those who have undergone healthy spiritual formation. This unit deals with the essentials of the missionary's spiritual formation and the resulting effects of this formation upon the mission of the church. (While this unit is approached with the missionary specifically in view, the principles of spiritual development presented here are equally applicable to the entire church who, after all, are all called to fulfill the mission of God.)

First, attention is given to the place of the Cross in the spiritual development of the missionary. Then, the distinctive Pentecostal understanding of the baptism in the Holy Spirit is presented as foundational to missions. The development of the devotional habit is treated as a necessity within the life of the missionary. The concept of missionary calling is explored in relationship to accomplishing the missionary task. And since missions relates to the world of people, consideration is given to personal and social formation. Only after this foundation of spiritual formation has been carefully laid is the missionary task then defined.

For the *missio Dei* to be accomplished within our time, the Church needs the spiritual development and growth consistent with its missionary vocation. Throughout this unit, the goal is to enable the reader to understand and realize a spiritual vitality, a vitality that is sometimes wistfully relegated to the pages of missions biography. The missionary role then becomes a continual quest to encourage the entire church, both at home and abroad, to see itself as the missionary people of God.

Spiritual formation is therefore at the heart of the missionary task and missions in the age of the Spirit.

Chapter 10:

Spiritual Formation in the Light of the Cross

The Centrality of the Cross

To be saved, one must " 'believe in the Lord Jesus' " (Acts 16:31). Believing implies hearing the gospel and calling " 'on the name of the *Lord*' " (Rom. 10:13). It is associated with repentance (Mark 1:15) and testified to by water baptism (Mark 16:16; Acts 2:38). Paul's summary of the gospel in 1 Corinthians 15:3–4 includes the death, burial, and resurrection of Christ. "For what I received I passed on to you as of first importance: that Christ died for our sins according to the Scriptures, that he was buried, that he was raised on the third day according to the Scriptures."

The death and resurrection of Christ are thus central to the gospel—the indispensable core without which there is no gospel. Since the death of Christ took place on a cross, the cross serves as the primary symbol of the Christian faith. The cross, however, is far more than simply a historic event or an artistic emblem or logo. It serves as a paradigm of the Christian life for all who truly follow Jesus.

Jesus repeatedly appealed to "taking up the cross" as the foundational requisite for any who would follow Him. In Matthew 10:37–38 Jesus states that anyone who loved father, mother, son, or daughter more than Him was not worthy of Him, " 'and anyone who does not take his cross and follow me is not worthy of me.' " In

Matthew 16:24 self-denial is linked with cross-bearing as essential for one who would follow Jesus. Mark 8:34 and Luke 9:23 are parallel references, with Luke's account specifying that the cross must be borne daily.

Jesus' statement " 'Whoever wants to save his life will lose it, but whoever loses his life for me will find it' " is given in Matthew 16:25; Mark 8:35; Luke 9:24; and in slightly different form in Matthew 10:39; Luke 14:26; 17:33; and John 12:25. Indeed, as one writer concludes, "No other saying of Jesus is given such emphasis."[1] In most cases, this insistence upon losing one's life in order to save it immediately follows an injunction to take up one's cross.

The inescapable conclusion is that Jesus taught that those who would follow Him were to love Him to the point of giving their lives for Him if necessary. He would be the center of their living and might become the cause of their dying. Self-centered living, even if apparently benign, was to have no place among His followers. Jesus' terms of service are such that no one following Him can live a life ultimately centered upon self, family, houses, lands, comforts, familiar circumstances, social advancement, security, or even fulfillment in ministry.

An unhealthy focus upon self and family is difficult to identify, because it tends to hide behind biblically mandated areas of concern. The context of Jesus' warning in Matthew 10 is that a man's foes will be from his own household (v. 36). Though a godly concern for one's family is vitally important, the ultimate benefit parents can bequeath to their children is a passionate concern to fulfill God's mission. Jesus repeatedly warns emphatically against anything that would take away from this passion. "The question whether one loves father or mother more than Christ is put to the test in

---

[1]Kenneth L. Barker, ed., *The NIV Study Bible* (Grand Rapids: Zondervan Publishing House, 1985), 1557.

any case in which the wishes of parents stand opposed to the known will of Christ."[2]

One might think that those who give themselves to Christian service, especially cross-cultural missionary service, would be immune to excessive attachment to houses, lands, or comforts. Unfortunately, this is not the case. Mission leaders often lament the inordinate amount of time given to resolve conflict concerning housing, automobiles, and other peripheral issues. Dr. Ajith Fernando, a noted Sri Lankan evangelical leader, observes, "If Christians do not regard suffering as part-and-parcel of servanthood and the centrality of the cross is downplayed, then their pain will be unduly increased because of these prevailing wrong attitudes. By trying to avoid suffering some will forsake God's call."[3]

The issues of social advancement, security, and fulfillment in ministry are closely related. All relate to the universal human desire for significance. Significance is measured both by external measurements, such as recognition or reward, and by internal measurements, such as the sense of fulfillment. Dr. Fernando refers to "fulfillment in ministry" as "a concept drawn from the secular idea of job satisfaction rather than from the biblical theology of the cross."[4] It is not that a follower of Christ never has a sense of fulfillment. Rather, the follower of the crucified Christ serves faithfully even through the periods when the sense of fulfillment is either slight or absent. It is at the end of the road that the disciple will hear the promised words " ' "Well done, good and faithful servant!" ' " (Matt. 25:21,23).

Of course, the paradox is that what one relinquishes often is returned as a gift from God accompanying a life

---

[2]John A. Broadus, *Commentary on Matthew* (Philadelphia: American Baptist Publication Society, [1866?]; Grand Rapids: Kregel Publications, 1990), 232 (page citations are to reprint edition).
[3]Ajith Fernando, "Is Western Christian Training Neglecting the Cross?" *Trinity World Forum* 24 (fall 1998): 5.
[4]Ibid., 4.

dedicated to His service. Jesus said, " 'No one who has left home or brothers or sisters or mother or father or children or fields for me and the gospel will fail to receive a hundred times as much in this present age (homes, brothers, sisters, mothers, children and fields—and with them, persecutions) and in the age to come, eternal life' " (Mark 10:29–30; see also Matt. 19:16–30; Luke 18:18–30).

Three observations should be made from these texts. First, Jesus demands total love and total obedience. Those who would follow Him must surrender unconditionally the rule of their lives to Him. They will not direct their lives according to personal preference. This is not to say that followers of Christ are to be characterized by thick clouds of mysticism. Of all people, they will be able to think reasonably as they plan to fulfill the stewardship of life. The Lord often makes His will known through rather ordinary processes of evaluation. He also may make clear to His followers that He is allowing them to make certain choices according to personal preference. Within a church or a missions organization, the will of God also may be made known or confirmed through a committee or a council (Acts 15:28), or through the directive of an administrative superior (Titus 1:5). Ultimately, however the Lord makes His will known, it is the Lord who must be the final authority to be unconditionally obeyed. Those who would follow Christ will earnestly seek to know His will as they make choices concerning such issues as ministry, employment, residence, personal safety, and lifestyle.

Since Christ cannot deny himself (2 Tim. 2:13), individual determinations of the will of God should be seen in the light of the revealed plan of God for humankind. All nations will be blessed through Jesus Christ, the offspring of Abraham (Gen. 12:3; 18:18; 22:18; Gal. 3:8,16). Jesus is the rightful ruler over God's eternal Kingdom (2 Sam. 7:16; Matt. 1:1; 28:18; Rev.

11:15). Believers will find their place in God's Kingdom primarily through their participation within the community of faith, the church (Matt. 16:18; Eph. 2:10–22; 3:6,10; 1 Tim. 3:15; 1 Pet. 2:9–10). Believers serve as witnesses of their belief in the crucified and risen Christ and His absolute authority to rule throughout the universe, now, in the future, and through all eternity.

Those who bear this witness live as Jesus taught in such chapters as Matthew 5. They identify with suffering, meekness, and peace-making (Matt. 5:4,5,9). They also rejoice in the face of unjust persecution (Matt. 5:11–12) as they serve as both salt and light within the world (Matt. 5:13–14).

Second, their Lord, who cares for His people as only a loving father and shepherd can, delights in giving the totally obedient blessing upon blessing, far more bountiful and of higher quality than they could have possibly demanded had they been in charge of their lives. The blessings, however, are not owned, nor are they entitlements. Rather, they are the gracious gifts of God upon the children of His love (Ps. 103:13; Matt. 6:31–33; John 1:16; Rom. 8:32; Phil. 4:19; 1 John 3:1).

Third, persecutions and other forms of difficulty will characterize this age. Jesus said, " 'In this world you will have trouble' " (John 16:33). Paul wrote, "In fact, everyone who wants to live a godly life in Christ Jesus will be persecuted" (2 Tim. 3:12). The children of darkness have always persecuted the children of light, and they will continue to do so until the end of the age (1 Cor. 2:8; Gal. 4:29; Eph. 6:10–12; 2 Tim. 3:13). No fact is more typical of present-day Christianity worldwide than the unreasonable and often blatant mistreatment of Christians.[5]

---

[5]See Paul Marshall with Lela Gilbert, *Their Blood Cries Out: The Worldwide Tragedy of Modern Christians Who Are Dying For Their Faith* (Dallas: Word, 1997); James Hefley and Marti Hefley, *By Their Blood*, 2d ed. (Grand Rapids: Baker Book House, 1996).

In addition to overt persecution, less aggressive forms of deprivation often result as well from the choice to follow Jesus. At times, Christians face discrimination in employment, education, or housing. They must be prepared to accept less-than-optimal circumstances as a matter of joyful obedience to their Lord. Preoccupation with possessions and comforts, position and power simply do not harmonize with the lifestyle of one who takes seriously Jesus' command to "deny yourself, take up your cross, and follow me."

Churches will, of course, enjoy times of peace (Acts 9:31). Believers need to learn, like Paul, to be "content in any and every situation." He said, "I know what it is to be in need, and I know what it is to have plenty. I have learned the secret of being content in any and every situation, whether well fed or hungry, whether living in plenty or in want. I can do everything through him who gives me strength" (Phil. 4:12–13).

However, when it comes to following Christ, even in times of peace there will always be a cross. To believe anything else is to be deceived. To prepare for anything less is to be unprepared. To experience anything less is an indication of failure.

Proclaiming the Cross

The representative of Jesus Christ must always remain focused upon the Cross as the center of all Christian proclamation. The following verses show that Paul regarded preaching the gospel as proclaiming the message of the Cross: "For Christ did not send me to baptize, but to preach the gospel—not with words of human wisdom, lest the cross of Christ be emptied of its power. For the message of the cross is foolishness to those who are perishing, but to us who are being saved it is the power of God" (1 Cor. 1:17–18).

It logically follows that all who would preach the gospel must deliver the message of the Cross.

Numerous texts demonstrate that the message of the Cross refers primarily to the atonement provided by Jesus Christ through His death and resurrection. A secondary message, taught by Jesus himself, extends the cross metaphorically to the life of self-sacrifice characteristic of all true followers of Him. No one can claim to be a preacher of the gospel without proclaiming both the redemption provided through Christ's death and a subsequent life of personal sacrifice consistent with Christ's command to "Take up your cross."

In Galatians, Paul identifies the cross as the cause of persecution: "Brothers, if I am still preaching circumcision, why am I still being persecuted? In that case the offense of the cross has been abolished. . . . Those who want to make a good impression outwardly are trying to compel you to be circumcised. The only reason they do this is to avoid being persecuted for the cross of Christ" (Gal. 5:11; 6:12).

To Paul, the cross had become symbolic of his renunciation of what he called "the world." He wrote, "May I never boast except in the cross of our Lord Jesus Christ, through which the world has been crucified to me, and I to the world" (Gal. 6:14).

In Ephesians, Paul lays the basis for New Testament ecclesiology. Christ's means for uniting Jew and Gentile in one body, not surprisingly, is the cross. "His purpose was to create in himself one new man out of the two, thus making peace, and in this one body to reconcile both of them to God through the cross, by which he put to death their hostility" (Eph. 2:15b–16).

In Philippians, the cross of Jesus represents the ultimate in humility: "And being found in appearance as a man, he humbled himself and became obedient to death—even death on a cross!" (Phil. 2:8). Of those refusing a life of self sacrifice, Paul wrote, "Many live as enemies of the cross of Christ" (Phil. 3:18).

Paul strongly warned the Colossians against the incipient Gnosticism then prevalent. It was Christ and not a mysterious experience that provided reconciliation for all things, and He did it "through his blood, shed on the cross" (Col. 1:20). The crucifixion also provided freedom from the penalty resulting from breaking God's law: "When you were dead in your sins and in the uncircumcision of your sinful nature, God made you alive with Christ. He forgave us all our sins, having canceled the written code, with its regulations, that was against us and that stood opposed to us; he took it away, nailing it to the cross. And having disarmed the powers and authorities, he made a public spectacle of them, triumphing over them by the cross" (Col. 2:13–15).

The author of Hebrews included himself in exhorting his readers, "Let us fix our eyes on Jesus, the author and perfecter of our faith, who for the joy set before him endured the cross, scorning its shame, and sat down at the right hand of the throne of God" (Heb. 12:2).

The cross, then, was the focal point of New Testament preaching. It served as the center of the gospel message being proclaimed, and it served as the constant reminder to those who would proclaim Christ that their model of ministry must always be the crucified Christ.

Implications of the Cross

To meet Jesus is to see Him carry His cross to Calvary, die for the sins of the world, and then rise from the dead—with power adequate "to save completely those who come to God through him" (Heb. 7:25). Jesus warned about those who would try to enter the sheepfold by some other way (John 10:1). Christian "conversion" that bypasses the cross (1) omits repentance, (2) encourages no real belief, and (3) provides no stable foundation for Christian service.

These three major implications of the cross should be in view from the moment of salvation:

First, the cross speaks of the punishment for sin. Scripture uniformly teaches that sin is a terrible affront to a holy God. "God is a righteous judge, a God who expresses his wrath every day" (Ps. 7:11). Christ's death was substitutionary in that He took upon himself the punishment for the sins of the world (Isa. 53:5,10; 2 Cor. 5:21) in order to become " 'Savior of the world' " (John 4:42, 1 John 4:14). This punishment demonstrates the gravity and consequence of human sinfulness. The believer remembers this punishment each time the sacramental meal is observed (1 Cor. 11:26). The believer also remembers the punishment for sin that awaits those who refuse God's offer of divine grace (Matt. 3:12; Mark 9:42–48; Heb. 10:26–31; Jude 14–15; Rev. 20:11–15; 21:8).

Second, we see the scope of what took place upon the cross. That Christ died for all is stated in 2 Corinthians 5:14, "For Christ's love compels us, because we are convinced that one died for all, and therefore all died." The resulting obligation to serve is stated in verse 15: "He died for all, that those who live should no longer live for themselves but for Him who died for them and was raised again." The Spirit of Christ within believers longs for the proclamation of the gospel to all the inhabited earth. Until that task is completed, each mention of the cross impels the believer to renewed witness to all the earth, since Christ died for all. Similarly, in 1 John 2:2–3, Christ's death for the sins of the whole world serves as the logical foundation for the believer's obligation to obey His commands: "He is the atoning sacrifice for our sins, and not only for ours but also for the sins of the whole world. We know that we have come to know him if we obey his commands." The commands immediately in focus following Christ's passion in the Gospels are the commands to make disciples of all nations and to receive the enduement of power (Matt. 28:19–20; Luke 24:46–49; Acts 1:4,8). The cross thus allows the believer to identify with Christ's worldwide mission in anticipation of the successful completion of the transferred apostolate (John 20:21).

Third, the cross speaks of new life, for its message

carries the prospect of resurrection. The old has passed away, and all things have become new (2 Cor. 5:17). We have been crucified with Christ, yet we live (Gal. 2:20). Because we are raised with Christ, we set our affections on those things that are above (Col. 3:1–2). The resurrection life has brought us new allegiance, new joy, a new family, and a new mission. Through the punishment of the cross, Christ provided a single plan of salvation to be shared by all believers (Acts 4:12; Jude 3). Through the same cross, all believers likewise share a common invitation to service: " 'If anyone would come after me, he must deny himself and take up his cross and follow me' " (Matt. 16:24). The blindness and misdirection of the former life are replaced by the clear vision of a mind fixed on things above. Such a resurrected life affords a logical basis for a moral imperative to disciple all nations.

Transformational Discipleship

The Church will transform the world to the degree that its people practice radical discipleship. To be world-changers, believers must first know they have passed from death to life. Then, they must be dissatisfied enough with a given state of affairs to bring about change.

First, since each believer is part of the "all" for whom Christ died (2 Cor. 5:14), the believer must accept personally the full transformational power of the Cross. In the words of 2 Corinthians 5:17, "Therefore, if anyone is in Christ, he is a new creation; the old has gone, the new has come!" Because of the cross, the disciple need not feel victimized by past sins or injustices, whether one's own, someone else's, or the combined sin and rebellion of one's ancestors. For "'if the Son sets you free, you will be free indeed'" (John 8:36). The Christ of the cross has conquered everything, bringing a freedom to serve that attracts others.

Second, the disciple is strongly aggrieved by the injustice, selfishness, and reckless pursuit of pleasure characterizing the kingdom of darkness. This aversion to evil is first of all demonstrated by a transformed personal lifestyle. "For what do righteousness and wickedness have in common? Or what fellowship can light have with darkness?" (2 Cor. 6:14b). In the words of Peter, "Therefore, since Christ suffered in his body, arm yourselves also with the same attitude, because he who has suffered in his body is done with sin" (1 Pet. 4:1). Or, as Paul tells the Romans, "count yourselves dead to sin but alive to God in Christ Jesus" (Rom. 6:11). While snatching some from the fire, the believer is "hating even the clothing stained by corrupted flesh" (Jude 23). Believers "have crucified the sinful nature with its passions and desires" (Gal. 5:24). They identify with Paul when he wrote, "May I never boast except in the cross of our Lord Jesus Christ, through which the world has been crucified to me, and I to the world" (Gal. 6:14). They keep the Lord's commandments—which they do not find burdensome because they have overcome the world through their faith (1 John 5:3–5).

In short, the magnet of the present social order has lost its hold on believers who have set their affections on things above (Col. 3:1). As a Nigerian pastor once said, "It takes a crucified someone to preach a crucified Christ."[6] As a believer, the missionary is a pilgrim and identifies with Peter's audience when he writes about their former acquaintances who "think it strange that you do not plunge with them into the same flood of dissipation, and they heap abuse on you" (1 Pet. 4:4).

The missionary is essentially separate from the present world order, a citizen of the coming Kingdom, which has already invaded the present world and is soon to come in fullness of power (Phil. 3:20). The

---

[6]Amos Emang, Eastern Nigeria Bible Institute chapel, Ogoja, Nigeria, [1976?].

transformation that missionaries bring to the present world order comes precisely because of their overriding allegiance to Christ's kingdom. Hence, the life of the missionary is characterized by a devotional habit, which is marked on the one hand by prayer and praise and on the other by the serious and systematic study of the Word of God. In this way, the controlling command of the Kingdom is realized: " 'Love the Lord your God with all your heart . . . soul . . . mind, and . . . strength' " (Mark 12:30). Only with this priority in place can the missionary hope to fulfill the second commandment, " ' "Love your neighbor as yourself" ' " (Mark 12:31).

The missionary task focuses upon building up the church as a community of the King, a fellowship of the crucified. The influence of the church then extends outward to those near and far. It is the nature of the church to bring the benefits of education to society, to minister compassionately to the hungry and sick, and to represent God's concern for humankind through serving as salt and light, especially in environments of exploitation and dehumanization. Upon one's love for God is built one's love for his neighbor, made in the image of God. The missionary's life is characterized by selfless sharing however and wherever needed. Such is the nature of radical discipleship.

It is absolutely essential to understand that the separation so strongly taught in the New Testament is in no way a separation from identification with the suffering, the abused, and the unprotected. Though delivered from the evil world system, the believer reaches back into the world to touch human suffering. No one was ever more free from the world than Christ; at the same time no one ever more willingly and fully penetrated the world with redemptive love. The same voluntary separation from the world system while identifying with its victims must characterize Christ's apostles. It is because they are not of the world (John 15:19) that they are able so compellingly and effectively to love people who need Christ's deliverance from the bondage of this world. This separation is also at the root of the persecution they must endure (John 15:20) even as they recommend the gospel, performing the "greater works" that Christ said those with faith in Him would perform (John 14:12, KJV). It is the separated, persecuted church that provides the atmosphere for these "greater works" that give testimony to the presence of the King.

STUDY QUESTIONS

1. What three observations does the text make concerning Christ's teaching of the cross? Interact with these points and make your own evaluative statement concerning the centrality of the cross in the teaching of Jesus.
2. Describe the place of the cross within the teaching of the Epistles. Give specific examples.
3. Comment upon the three implications of the cross given in the text.
4. Describe the "separation/identification paradox" that serves as the basis for radical discipleship.

Chapter 11:
Holy Spirit Baptism

Power for Service

If salvation and its consequent commitment to a life of radical discipleship form the foundation of Christian service, the baptism in the Holy Spirit provides the power for that service. Most Christians would agree that an infusion of the Spirit's power is basic to a life of service; the Pentecostal contribution is the emphasis that this empowerment is subsequent to salvation, that the believer is baptized in the Holy Spirit after having been saved. Christ's command in Acts 1:4–5 is understood to be normative for the entire Church until He returns: "On one occasion, while he [Jesus] was eating with them, he gave them [His disciples] this command: 'Do not leave Jerusalem, but wait for the gift my Father promised, which you have heard me speak about. For John baptized with water, but in a few days you will be baptized with the Holy Spirit.'"

Though a detailed consideration of the traditional Pentecostal position on the subsequence of Spirit baptism is beyond the scope of this text, the following points should be noted:

1. The promise of the Holy Spirit's indwelling (John 14:17) was realized when Jesus breathed on the disciples and said, " 'Receive the Holy Spirit' " (John 20:22). It was after this that Jesus directed the disci-

ples, " 'Wait for the gift my Father promised' " (Acts 1:4). This is consistent with the view that the baptism in the Holy Spirit is an impartation of power subsequent to the indwelling of the Spirit experienced by all New Testament believers.

2. Throughout the Book of Acts, an enduement of power remained normative for the Church. This in seen in Samaria (Acts 8), in the Cornelius account (Acts 10; 11), and in Ephesus (Acts 19). In Acts 8 and 19 this impartation of power came with the laying on of hands, while in Acts 10 it came spontaneously while the gospel was being preached. In Acts 8 the enduement of power is clearly subsequent to salvation. In Acts 19:2 the aorist participle *pisteusantes* (from the verb for "believe") may indicate action prior to the action of the main verb. In that case, Acts 19 would support subsequence, that is, an enduement of power subsequent to salvation.

The argument for subsequence, however, does not depend on this interpretation of the participle. Even if *pisteusantes* is taken to have the same time reference as the main verb, as is sometimes the case with the aorist participle, the coming of the Spirit may be viewed as being basically simultaneous without being the same event as believing.[1] This appears to be what happened in Acts 10 (recounted in Acts 11). As the hearers listened to Peter present the gospel, they believed (one experience) and were simultaneously filled with the Holy Spirit (a separate though simultaneous experience).

3. This empowerment is an enablement of supernatural power to fulfill Christ's commission to disciple the nations. That this is to be the agenda of the Church until Christ returns is shown by the empower-

---

[1]For a discussion of the aorist participle as used in Acts 19, see Stanley M. Horton, *Acts,* vol. 6 of *The Complete Biblical Library: The New Testament* (Springfield, Mo.: World Library Press, 1991), 449.

ment/nations/return development of thought within Acts 1:8–10: " 'But you will receive power when the Holy Spirit comes on you; and you will be my witnesses in Jerusalem, and in all Judea and Samaria, and to the ends of the earth.' After he said this, he was taken up before their very eyes, and a cloud hid him from their sight. They were looking intently up into the sky as he was going, when suddenly two men dressed in white stood beside them. 'Men of Galilee,' they said, 'why do you stand here looking into the sky? This same Jesus, who has been taken from you into heaven, will come back in the same way you have seen him go into heaven.' "

Divine Enablement and Confidence

In practical terms, this means that the Pentecostal missionary approaches the task confident that the power (Gk. *dunamis*) of the Holy Spirit, received when one is baptized in the Holy Spirit, will be adequate for every challenge. There is no need to hesitate in personal witness, public preaching, exercise of spiritual gifts, or direct confrontation with the powers of darkness.

The Pentecostal missionary's confidence rests primarily upon the power imparted at the time of being baptized in the Holy Spirit; Jesus' statement linking Pentecostal power with the exercise of worldwide witness is foundational (Acts 1:8). In addition to the natural abilities and gifts that have been discovered in the course of ministry, the Pentecostal missionary also earnestly desires "the greater gifts" (1 Cor. 12:31), knowing that there is abundant divine enablement for those who move forward in obedience to God's will (1 Cor. 12:11; Eph. 4:7). It naturally follows that the Pentecostal missionary expects to operate in the realm of the supernatural.

Occasionally, a Pentecostal believer may feel his or her experience of the baptism in the Holy Spirit is inadequate, and must grapple with this. Honestly facing such feelings will create an insatiable hunger for God's presence—so necessary for the accomplishment of God's mission. In addition to Acts 1:8, the believer remembers key promises such as the following:

> "For I will pour water on the thirsty land, and streams on the dry ground; I will pour out my Spirit on your offspring, and my blessing on your descendants" (Isa. 44:3).
>
> "And afterward, I will pour out my Spirit on all people. Your sons and daughters will prophesy, your old men will dream dreams, your young men will see visions. Even on my servants, both men and women, I will pour out my Spirit in those days" (Joel 2:28–29).
>
> "Blessed are those who hunger and thirst for righteousness, for they will be filled" (Matt. 5:6).
>
> "Which of you fathers, if your son asks for a fish, will give him a snake instead? Or if he asks for an egg, will give him a scorpion? If you then, though you are evil, know how to give good gifts to your children, how much more will your Father in heaven give the Holy Spirit to those who ask him!" (Luke 11:11–13).

While the quest for God is life-long, the believer must come to a humbling but empowering experience of the baptism in the Holy Spirit. To fail at this point is to back away from the only power adequate to meet the challenge of Christ's mandate. The Church is weakened and its ultimate result inadequate if missionaries operate with less than an overflowing experience of the baptism in the Holy Spirit.

Further Concerns

Two further concerns should also be addressed. First, the baptism in the Holy Spirit is not to be equated with either emotionalism or some other human reaction to the Spirit's presence. Human personalities are different, and learned responses vary. What is essential is the reality of the impartation of divine power focused in witness and service. There are those who equate Pentecostalism with exuberance in worship or emotional behavior. While it would be unwise to belittle the significance of human emotions or lively worship patterns, these are not the essence of Pentecostalism. The heart of Pentecostalism is the supernatural empowerment of believers so that they may, in word and deed, adequately bear witness of Christ to the nations of the world.

Second, the matter of speaking in tongues needs to be addressed. The occurrence of speaking in tongues in Acts was "remarkable" in that it was highly noticeable and became the object of agitated discussion (Acts 2:7–12). It was also "evidential" because it was the most telling evidence Peter could appeal to in defense of his having baptized Gentiles (Acts 10:44–48; 11:15–17). Pentecostal believers worldwide notice the same two functions within the contemporary spread of the gospel. The supernatural, including such manifestations as healings and speaking in tongues, is still remarkable to vast numbers of people. Around the world, crowds still rush together asking, "What does this mean?" Further, speaking in tongues is still evidential as it occurs within the context of Christian worship. I mention the Christian context, because there may be a demonic imitation. In my experience, for example, a woman under demonic power who knew no English once spoke to me in English. However, when the gospel is preached and believers seek to be filled with the Holy Spirit, the entire church knows they have been filled when they begin to worship God in other tongues. This phenomenon is typical worldwide within contexts of Pentecostal worship, and it is the primary reason why seemingly ordinary men and women become powerful witnesses of Christ.

It would appear fitting as something of an antithesis to the phenomenon at Babel, that those empowered to represent Christ among the nations of the world should receive their enduement of power with the accompanying sign of speaking in the languages of the world. As Don Richardson observes, "Seen in the context of Jesus' ministry and His clearly articulated plans for the whole world, the bestowal of that miraculous outburst of *Gentile* languages could have only one main purpose: . . . the evangelization of all peoples."[2]

At times, friendly non-Pentecostals ask Pentecostals if they have relaxed their emphasis upon evidential tongues. Such questions usually focus upon doctrinal discussion or worship practice without relating them to *missio Dei* and the Church. What should be noted, however, is the correlation between speaking in tongues and the resulting experience of Christian witness, especially among those of diverse ethnicity and language. As long as there is a hurting and broken world divided primarily along lines of language and ethnicity, I hope Pentecostals will increase their emphasis upon speaking in tongues. It would be an untold tragedy to back away from that part of our heritage that most directly gives evidence of God's determination to bless all nations through Christ, the seed of Abraham (Gal. 3:16).

Unfortunately, the Pentecostal position has occasionally been the source of debate, or even division. The Pentecostal agenda, however, is not typically one of controversy. Rather, it is the agenda of the Spirit—the agenda of the people of God moving in the power of God to accomplish the mission of God (*missio Dei*) among all made in the image of God. In common with the Book of Acts, modern Pentecostals report mighty outpourings of the Holy Spirit, including spontaneous instances of speaking in tongues that result in both planned and unplanned evangelism, especially among the poor, including those of wide ethnic and linguistic diversity. Those who are hungry are still invited to partake that they, too, may become participants in missions in the age of the Spirit.

---

[2]Don Richardson, *Eternity in Their Hearts* (Ventura, Calif.: Regal Books, 1981), 157, Richardson's emphasis.

STUDY QUESTIONS

1. Describe the biblical basis of the enduement of power that is basic to a Pentecostal theology of ministry. Comment on your understanding of the relevant texts.
2. Comment on speaking in tongues as an evidence of divine concern for the nations of the world.

Chapter 12:
Devotional Habit

Students often ask their teachers for suggestions that will lead to a successful missionary career. While the context of these questions is often leadership skills, cross-cultural sensitivity, or ministry development, the real secret to representing the Kingdom well is one's maintaining a healthy relationship with the King. This is done primarily through making a healthy devotional life a priority. Succeeding at this point is the key to everything a missionary hopes to accomplish. There is no substitute for a deep personal relationship with God, which results from habitual fellowship with Him and obedient response to his Word. Failing at this point separates the servant from the will of his Master, rendering even sacrificial service anemic and devoid of blessing. The baptism in the Holy Spirit is never a substitute for the discipline of devotion. Rather, devotion is the atmosphere in which the power of the Holy Spirit operates to accomplish *missio Dei* in the earth.

The pressures of life and ministry often impinge upon the quality and quantity of the missionary's personal times of spiritual enrichment. To encourage the devotional habit as of first importance, it is developed here at some length, under two headings. First, several benefits of maintaining an adequate devotional life will be considered. Then, several insights will be given on how to realize devotional objectives.

Benefits of the Devotional Habit

1. A BIBLICAL WORLDVIEW

The effects of social environment often show up in an individual's basic assumptions about life. On the one hand, the environment contributes to a rich cultural diversity. On the other hand, however, social pressures may predispose an individual toward nonscriptural outlooks on the issues of the day.

The two essential components of a personal devotional habit are Bible study and prayer. Ideally, these two are enriched through song, the reading of other devotional materials, and personal reflection (such as is done when one writes). Discussion may also enrich one's devotions, through sharing with someone either at the time of devotion or later, perhaps in a classroom.

The Christian views the Bible as "inspired" (see 2 Tim. 3:16; Gk. *theopneustos,* "God-breathed"). In common with many other Christians, Pentecostals typically believe this inspiration is "verbal and plenary," meaning that the very words of the entire autograph of the Bible are inspired. For such believers, the operative question in any situation becomes, "What does the Bible say?" The Bible is held to speak to issues of theology, moral values, and the great questions of life. For example, the Bible speaks of the purpose of God within His creation, the purpose of the Church, and the purpose of individual existence. It describes the role and responsibilities of the individual with respect to the family, the church, the community, the state, and the stranger, or foreigner.

Approaching the Christian life without an adequate means of comprehending the message of the Bible makes one vulnerable to forming values and making decisions based on public opinion. Even if such persons are true believers, their contribution to the advance of the kingdom of God may be minimized. How can one contribute meaningfully to a cause that is only vaguely understood?

The first benefit of a consistent devotional habit, then, is the realization of a worldview that takes the message of the Scriptures seriously. Though serious Christians may not agree on all current issues, those who habitually read the Bible tend to hold common assumptions about life. When faced with life's choices, their instinctive points of reference become the persons, events, and statutes of Scripture. This approach to life directly affects how a missionary contributes to the completion of the task. Only as missionaries stay under the tutelage of the Word do they have hope of reflecting and representing Kingdom values cross-culturally.

Those lacking a consistent diet of the Scriptures, by contrast, most naturally tend to build their value structures from news or entertainment media, the opinions of friends and family, or other sources within the local environment.

2. AN ANCHOR

How is a missionary to stay calm and secure when the circumstances of life seem to be a howling gale? Emotional, mental, physical, and spiritual attacks often result in paralyzing and debilitating fear. V. Raymond Edman has advised, "Danger feared is folly, danger faced is freedom."[1] But how can personal danger be faced effectively?

In Revelation 22:6, the angel said to John, "'These words are trustworthy and true.'" A major purpose of personal devotions is to deepen the conviction that God's Word is true. On the one hand, the missionary absolutely believes that God's plan for history will take place exactly as He said it would: with those from every nation, tribe, people and language worshiping Christ. Even the hardest field must yield to His lordship. On the other hand, the missionary absolutely believes that no personal circum-

---

[1] V. Raymond Edman, *The Disciplines of Life* (Minneapolis: World Wide Publications, 1948), 23.

stance—no pain, no loneliness, no misunderstanding, no spiritual battle—can remove the certainty that God is in control of his life, loves him, and is pleased with his love for Him. This hope is "an anchor for the soul" (Heb. 6:19). It is firm and secure and will keep the missionary stable and productive in the midst of every trial.

The belief that Christ's Word is trustworthy and true dispels fear that focuses on the impossible and the unknown, for God is the God of both. The believer lies prostrate at the feet of Jesus as did John in Revelation, indicating total submission, knowing that if He allows suffering, it is for a limited time. Faced obediently, trials only make us grow more like Christ. There is no possibility of being abandoned or of prayer being ineffectual. The believer is so closely identified with God that an offense against the believer is an offense against God and will be avenged by God himself (Zech. 2:8; Heb. 10:30). Nothing can snatch the believer from God's protective hand (John 10:28–29). The believer does not submit to fear, knowing that anything feared is temporal and, compared with eternity, meaningless. No present circumstance, no matter how threatening, can possibly take away from the truth of God's Word. The investment of a life for Jesus has eternal value. It is never wasted, never unnoticed, and, ultimately, never unrewarded.

He is Lord even during our bad days, and though the missionary is aware there is a cross to be borne, there is also the confident knowledge that after the cross comes the resurrection and the crown. Where fear reigns, there will be apathy, complacency, and discontent. Where Christ is in control, the paralysis of fear will give way to the activity of faith. Even in the midst of the hard times, "It is impossible to know Him, to love Him, to surrender to Him as Lord—and do *nothing!* His very presence flushes us out of our comfort zone, demanding and provoking activity!"[2]

---

[2]Anne Graham Lotz, *The Vision of His Glory* (Dallas: Word, 1996), 113, Lotz's emphasis.

3. GROWTH IN WORSHIP

Another benefit of a healthy devotional habit is growth in worship. God is worshiped only as well as He is known, and He is known primarily through His Word. As God is known better, worship choruses and hymns take on new meaning. The worshiper feels what the author of the song felt, and the heart responds in joyful adoration to the Lord.

Within a foreign context, local forms of worship are likewise meaningful because of a shared biblical worldview even though there may be little similarity in form or sound to the worship of the home country.

4. EFFECTIVE SUPPLICATION AND INTERCESSION

Many missionaries pray for the world systematically by using print and Internet materials on the progress of worldwide evangelization. These informational resources and prayer guides deal with the world country by country and are periodically updated. The progress of the gospel is tracked statistically and unreached people groups are described.

As the believer delights in knowing God and responding in praise to Him, a renewed ministry of prayer results. The missionary finds that supplication and intercession bring unity among colleagues sharing assignments. Hopefully, their prayers become centered on the kingdom of God (Matt. 6:33). Tears are shed over the needs of others. Then, inevitably, the shared joy of answered prayer brings a permanent bonding as nothing else can. When Christ's kingdom triumphs despite every adversity, those who shared in His sufferings become permanent family members with each other. There is no higher joy, a joy known only through prayer.

5. SHARED VISION

The parents in a missionary family often long for meaningful ways to share the joy of their calling with their children as well as with others who may be in their home. Family devotions provide the opportunity to work through the questions that are prompted by the daily readings or that are brought to the devotional time by participants. In this way parents share their vision with their children. Children learn how to pray by praying with their parents. They also learn by what they observe of their parents' private devotional lives, since they are well aware of the effects of extended times of personal renewal spent alone with God. Those who are single also have times of such sharing, for they often become close to national Christians and to other missionaries.

6. Something Significant to Teach

Missionaries who live in a continual search of God's Word grow in their understanding of it. They begin to realize that the same principles that helped in their personal development also apply to group development within any cultural milieu. In other words, their devotion to the Word has enabled them to contribute meaningfully to their new setting.

Daily time with the Word soon supplies a background that allows an individual to enjoy preparing for teaching opportunities. That is, those investing in a devotional time become familiar with the Bible's themes, how they are developed within the Bible's various parts, and how to lead others to the principles that will help them to apply the Bible to life.

The list of benefits from maintaining an adequate devotional life could go on and on. However, let me change the focus slightly for consideration of insights into how the devotional life may be approached so as to achieve these benefits. I want to consider both the view of devotions that will yield the benefits and some suggestions that may also prove helpful. A dozen insights follow.

Insights on the Devotional Habit

1. SEEING DEVOTIONS AS LOVING GOD

The key to establishing a healthy devotional life is to think of devotional time as an expression of your love for God. A teacher of the law once asked Jesus which was the most important of all the commandments. " 'The most important one,' answered Jesus, 'is this: "Hear, O Israel, the Lord our God, the Lord is one. Love the Lord your God with all your heart and with all your soul and with all your mind and with all your strength." The second is this: "Love your neighbor as yourself." There is no commandment greater than these' " (Mark 12:29–31).

The believer should be reading the Bible primarily out of love for God. The Bible reveals who God is and how the believer relates to God in heart, soul, mind, and strength. It also shows how the believer relates to people, who, after all, are made in God's image. It was when Adam sinned that he deliberately avoided a planned meeting with God (Gen. 3:8–10). However, the believer, knowing all sin is forgiven, joyfully anticipates the fellowship that occurs in Bible reading and response to the Word. There is added joy when, in those times of fellowship, the believer understands that the Savior also commissions the forgiven to lives of service. The missionary vocation is the response to such moments of spiritual intimacy between the forgiven and their Lord.

2. BECOMING AN "INSIDER"

One of the great problems of life is the sense many have that they do not belong. Immeasurable hurt comes throughout life to those who, for one reason or another, feel like outsiders. The social pressure to conform to group opinion is enormous, and the strength of that pressure corresponds to one's innate desire to be accepted. People are vulnerable to unwise decisions during times when the desire to be accepted is especially acute, such as is often the case during the teen years.

The missionary is especially susceptible to feelings of not belonging. During the early years of service, everything seems different, a condition commonly known as "culture shock."[3] It is as though a person approached his computer one morning to begin work and discovered that during the night all the default settings had been changed. But the worst part of the problem is not in things being different; missionaries expect this. The problem is more subtle. Not only is everything different, but all that is different seems to have united into an unfriendly system, in which the missionary is an outsider. The environment, in effect, has judged the missionary unworthy as a human being. With the judgment rendered, the duration of the term becomes a laboratory of experiments, each designed to support the judgment.

It would be bad enough if the terrible sense of being isolated came only from outsiders, that is, those outside the household of faith. Then the missionary would still feel okay and might even regard the social opinion makers as simply misguided. In fact, however, a worse sense of isolation comes from the perception that one is not accepted by fellow missionaries. Though they all mean well, they may seem to convey the message that the newly arrived are terribly out of step, that they do not belong. For example, they did not pack well, or they should not be emotionally stressed, or they should have their children under greater control. The missionary couple had thought they had life pretty well put together. Upon arrival, however, they feel challenged on the points they once viewed as strengths: Their

---

[3]For a helpful discussion of culture shock, see Marge Jones and E. Grant Jones, *Psychology of Missionary Adjustment* (Springfield, Mo.: Logion Press, 1995), 53–64.

dress is deemed inappropriate, their daily routine betrays lack of organization, their views are generally suspect. Instead of being the respected leaders, the new missionaries have been returned to the insecurities of their adolescence.

But the good news is that not everything has changed. God has not (Mal. 3:6)! Jesus Christ has not (Heb. 13:8)!

Missionaries undergoing any of the above symptoms require the affirmation of the Holy Spirit. And this affirmation comes primarily in times alone with God, hearing from Him through the Bible and responding to Him in worship. Those new missionaries able to maintain a systematic devotional habit will begin to feel that they belong and that everything will be all right. But those who look primarily to their missionary peers for affirmation, by contrast, will find their feelings soaring one day and plummeting the next.

Gaining a sense of belonging, the new missionary will realize that comments that had hurt were not intended to. To the contrary, they were intended to help. The other missionaries will seem okay after all. They will seem to be less threatening, or will even seem affirming, if only the new missionary's sense of belonging can grow.

Hopefully, the confidence of the new missionary will grow until even difficult advice will be welcomed. It was an older and wiser King David who wrote, "Let a righteous man strike me—it is a kindness; let him rebuke me—it is oil on my head. My head will not refuse it" (Ps. 141:5). This growth comes through the fellowship of the Holy Spirit, primarily as He speaks through the devotional times with the Word in the quiet place. Experiencing the Spirit's presence, the insecure missionary will change as a confidence comes from within. Others will sense this confidence, and the downward spiral will have ended.

3. REALIZING DEVOTIONAL OBJECTIVES DESPITE OBSTACLES

The secret to the devotional life is to follow a daily schedule that includes both personal and family devotions. These devotions should be approached as a spiritual discipline, something to be joyously anticipated and seriously planned for. At the same time, most missionaries will report that exceptions are to be expected; the key is to be sure that the exceptions do not become the rule. If the ox is daily found in the ditch, the owner might consider building a fence or buying a rope. Those who establish regular times of prayer while maturely coping with the exceptions will find immeasurable benefits, such as those listed above.

Some words of encouragement to those in special circumstances: Mothers of small children, for example, may find it impossible to retain previous devotional patterns. Often such mothers begin feeling "unspiritual" or even unworthy of the missionary vocation. Their level of discouragement seems to be proportionate to their previous level of spiritual growth, that is, the more faithful one was in previous times, the more deeply distressed in times of arrest. The first word of encouragement is that the God who specially loves children does not withhold that love from their mothers. Realize that Jesus understands and cares. In any case, it is nearly always counterproductive to indulge in self-recrimination.

As a further word of encouragement, devotions may be viewed as vitamins: They help best if taken daily in small dosages. If a mother usually reads several chapters of the Bible a day, she may find it necessary to read just one a day for a time. A long chapter such as Matthew 5 has 1,075 words and can be read comfortably in less than eleven minutes. Thankfully, such chapters also break down into sections, paragraphs, and sentences. Often the husband, older children, or household assistants can help in such a way that even a busy mother has fifteen or thirty minutes to herself for a quiet time with God. The husband will be supportive when he understands the importance of such a time and realizes that benefits are being lost by everyone when his wife cannot spend time alone with God.

Both husband and wife may have public ministry that requires preparation time. Such preparation tends to come all at once, such as when one is teaching, or taking, a block course. As much preparation as possible should be done early so that the devotional time will not be abandoned, though it may need to be restructured or abbreviated. Early planning may call for redistributing usual tasks in view of the temporary overloading facing either husband or wife. Happy is the couple who are aware of the need for temporary assistance from time to time and who actively support each other however needed. Do not make the mistake of assuming that a time budget is fixed, that no temporary overload can be considered. The healthy family build enough time margins into their schedule so that an extra course, or a revival meeting, or a business trip, or a foreign visitor is welcomed and does not pose insurmountable difficulties or occasion resentment.

A further word is in order concerning specially designated times of prayer, fasting, reading the Bible through, or other forms of spiritual discipline. A missionary husband and wife should share a level of spiritual fellowship that allows for such times of growth without their becoming a cause of misunderstanding. The purpose should be shared mutually and appropriate means of encouragement should follow so that the purpose is realized, even if only one of the spouses is observing the event.

4. Considering Study Bibles and Bible Versions

While I will not evaluate the many English study Bibles, Bible versions, and paraphrases that are available, I do want to comment on making the most of study Bibles and of gaining a working knowledge of at least the major versions.

First, it is important to have an English translation that becomes your standard to memorize and return to. This should be one that you feel comfortable with and, if possible, one that is acceptable to those among whom you work.

There are times in devotional reading that the missionary will prefer as clean a text as possible, without personal annotation or study helps. This practice is certainly helpful in reading quickly, in doing one's own critical thinking, and in prayerfully listening for the voice of the Holy Spirit. It would be an impoverishment, however, to permanently exclude study Bibles from one's diet. I would encourage missionaries to systematically read a study Bible until they have gleaned what it has to offer. Then, it would be helpful to try another study Bible for awhile. The treasury of scholarship and devotional material that may be absorbed in this way will give the reader a continually expanding knowledge of Scripture. *The Full Life Study Bible* is available in both the KJV and NIV and offers a wealth of study materials prepared by reputable Pentecostal scholars.[4] It is available in an increasing number of languages around the world. Numerous other study Bibles, representing distinct format, study methodology, and doctrinal perspective, are also available.

Most Bible readers find it helpful to read familiar passages in different translations, the greatest benefit being the additional meaning gained from the same passage. Reading a different translation from time to time tends to keep the reader alert and stimulate further study.

---

[4]Donald C. Stamps, ed., *The Full Life Study Bible* (Grand Rapids: Zondervan Publishing House, 1992).

In addition to reading the English text, many missionaries find it helpful to read systematically and devotionally from the language translation used most frequently by the believers they identify with. This practice supplies the missionary a much-needed common background with them as they face the questions of life. It also allows the missionary insights into the meaning of Scripture that might otherwise have been missed.

Others find it helpful to do at least a portion of their reading in the original languages (i.e., Hebrew and Greek). Those with this facility should be encouraged to keep their skills current. Unit II referred to the late Pentecostal missiologist Dr. Melvin Hodges. When I first heard him introduced in 1973 it was as the man who "reads devotionally from the Greek text." Perhaps his love for the Greek New Testament may help to explain some of his missiological insights.

There are several editions of the Bible designed to lead the reader through the whole of it in either one or two years. Or, an edition may combine Old and New Testament readings, covering, for example, the New Testament twice in two years and the Old Testament once. One may also check with a Bible society or a Christian bookseller about obtaining a Bible reading chart for keeping track of readings.

5. CONSIDERING DEVOTIONAL CLASSICS

I recommend devotional readings to others, because I know how blessed I have been by them. When I was ten years old, my parents gave me a leather-bound Bible for Christmas. This gift became the occasion for systematizing my personal Bible reading. I well remember the joy of finishing the entire Bible. Soon, other books followed, including devotional classics such as *The Journals of John Wesley* and *The Confessions of St. Augustine.* It was a special joy when for another Christmas, I received my very own Strong's Concordance. In junior high school, I discovered the writings of Elizabeth Elliott, and in high school I became especially fascinated with John Bunyan's *Pilgrim's Progress.* Though I did not realize it at the time, I was developing an appetite for both the Bible, and for classic and contemporary devotional materials. I am especially indebted to my parents for their role in developing my interest in reading such materials.

While in college, my devotional reading broadened. I remember being blessed through two gifts: Harry Ironside's devotional classic *The Daily Sacrifice,* and *Matthew Henry's Commentary.* While critical scholars may not be helped a great deal by Henry, Charles Spurgeon reportedly advised all young ministers to read completely his commentaries. Though I did not attain that ideal, reading Henry was good for me.

Later, a missions leader, Dr. Delmer Guynes, introduced our class of missionary candidates to the writings of A. B. Simpson[5] and F. J. Huegel.[6] Through the years, my wife and I have been blessed by devotional masterpieces written by such missionaries as Amy Carmichael, Isobel Kuhn, Hudson Taylor, and Mrs. Howard Taylor. Other devotional authors that have been helpful to us include Max Lucado, Phillip Keller, F. B. Meyer, Lloyd John Ogilvie, and Charles Swindoll. Helpful writers from a Pentecostal tradition have included Donald Gee, Stanley Horton, David Wilkerson, and Jack Hayford. Each of these writers has been used as an agent of God to strengthen our inner being, and we are deeply in their debt.

Individual tastes vary and some of the authors I have named are less known now than they once were. Still, the missionary who would be an ambassador for God would be well served by reading those God has used, both in the past as well as in the present.

---

[5]E.g., *A Larger Christian Life.*
[6]E.g., *Bone of His Bone; The Cross of Christ—The Throne of God.*

6. CONSIDERING ELECTRONIC ACCESS TO DEVOTIONAL MATERIAL

Missionaries should be aware of the Bible and devotional computer software programs that are available. These include entire libraries, complete with Hebrew and Greek texts, multiple Bible versions, devotional and critical commentaries, lexical aids, devotional classics, and hymns. Add to this the proliferation of excellent Christian videos, children's materials, and worship music, and one can see that a remarkable array of devotional materials is available electronically.

7. MAXIMIZING DEVOTIONAL BENEFIT THROUGH KEEPING A JOURNAL

Several years ago, I noticed that my teenage son was keeping a spiritual journal. This inspired me to do the same. I came to realize that keeping a journal encouraged the understanding and application of my Bible readings. Even if one does not often go back to reread entries, the discipline of condensing Bible readings or prayers into a journal entry makes them more memorable. Also, there is the added benefit that the Spirit's impressions upon one's heart are recorded as milestones, which might otherwise be forgotten.

To maximize the benefit of journaling, take the following steps. First, if writing by hand, procure a suitable journal; if writing by computer, set up an appropriate file. Random notes may help in a pinch, but there is no substitute for an orderly approach to a long-term project.

Second, determine the nature of the entries you want to make. I have found it helpful to record a summary statement for each chapter of Scripture read. A record of prayers and subsequent answers is also encouraging. This was the method used by my wife with our children when we were involved in opening a new Bible college many years ago in Nigeria. My wife kept the requests and answers on facing pages of a notebook: on the left page, the requests; and on the right, the answers—directly opposite the corresponding request. The effects of this method upon our son and daughter were amazing as they realized that God really was answering their prayers. Many of those who journal record their inner joys and sorrows. Some keep a running dialogue between themselves and God. Any method will work if it is approached systematically and sincerely.

Third, plan for periodic reflection. This could be weekly or monthly. Review what you have done with the intention of knowing God better, obeying Him, and sensing His direction through the sometimes mundane routines of duty.

Fourth, plan to share some special blessing or insight from your journal. You may easily gather choice nuggets and share them with someone special as you would share a sunrise, the fragrance of a flower, or the account of a recent holiday.

8. NOTING MILESTONES

Stone monuments in the Book of Joshua are significant. After crossing the Jordan River, Joshua (4:6) told the people that their children would ask about the significance of the stone monument he had erected (to which each tribe had contributed a stone from the river). The question was to occasion the retelling of the Lord's mighty act of opening the Jordan River at flood stage, allowing the Israelites to cross on dry ground. In Joshua 4:23 this miracle was likened to the earlier miracle of the crossing of the Red Sea. Stones also were used to demarcate tribal boundaries (see chs. 15; 18), to demonstrate the unity of the tribes on both sides of the Jordan (ch. 22), and as a witness of the renewed covenant (24:26).

In a similar way, the significant events of one's spiritual pilgrimage should be marked for future reference.

The New Testament gives ample witness that water baptism served as a sign of identification between the believer and the risen Lord. The baptism in the Holy Spirit within the Book of Acts definitely functioned as an unmistakable marker, both in the transition of the glory of God to the Church and in the identification of new believers with *missio Dei*.

Beyond keeping a journal, I would appeal for missionaries to symbolically "set up stone pillars" so that milestones are noted and remembered. While living in Nigeria, we became acquainted with the saying "No event, no history." The believer in Christ is in the business of noticing "events" of God within human history, especially as those events, or interventions, signal the progress of *missio Dei* toward its ultimate conclusion. Missionary parents have the signal opportunity and awesome privilege of identifying for their children signs of God's intervention in human affairs: Was a visa granted against all odds? Did unexpected finance enable the mission to continue? Was property granted despite impossibilities? Did protection occur in the face of a threat? Was there sudden recovery from serious illness? All such events need to be noted, interpreted so as to give God glory, and appropriately remembered.

Those who note milestones within their family will naturally move toward noting other milestones. In a Bible college, for example, an annual homecoming may provide far more than an occasion for fellowship and planning of the future. It may also be the occasion for a spiritual event based upon the shared recollection of miracles. Perhaps people would have less trouble believing God for miracles in times of distress if the obvious miracles of the past were more appropriately celebrated.

Missionaries, of all people, should become expert at planning for suitable recognition of the power of the Holy Spirit as evidenced in the accomplishment of their mission.

9. STUDY AS THE STEWARDSHIP OF REVELATION

Besides a significant devotional habit, ongoing study is also a necessity.

As a junior in high school, I was interested in the reason our Sunday school teacher gave for his teaching. He was a certified public accountant who owned a significant business, and I supposed it was unusual that he took the time to teach Sunday school. He explained that teaching requires Bible study, and that the personal benefits of this study were so great that he continued to teach. While that may not seem to be a student-centered reason for teaching, the value the teacher placed upon study made a deep impression upon me. Another deep impression about the value of study came to me from my father. He taught an adult Sunday school class for nineteen years, and I often marveled at how seriously he took this assignment as he routinely spent most of his Saturdays in preparation.

The scriptural teaching that God has revealed himself through His Word is basic to all Bible study (e.g., 2 Tim. 3:16). Several conclusions resting upon this premise are listed below.

- The missionary must make a habit of the serious study of the Word of God in addition to daily devotional readings. Extended times of study should be considered essential to a life dedicated to communicating the gospel to the lost and discipling the saved (Matt. 28:19; Luke 19:10). Since God is known primarily through his written Word and since both the lost and the found need to know that Word if they are to please God, those who would deliberately represent God to others must also know that Word.

- Since the Bible and related study materials are readily available, all believers should view themselves as stewards of such valuable resources. "So then, men ought to regard us as servants of Christ and as those entrusted with the secret things of God. Now it is required that those who have been given a trust must prove faithful" (1 Cor. 4:1–2).

- The serious study of the Word of God is a lifelong process. African wisdom says, "To become a man is not a one-day job." Likewise, to know God's Word well enough to communicate it to others is the job of a lifetime.

- The serious study of the Word of God should be the undertaking of *all* believers. It would be a mistake to relegate the study of the Bible to those with academic backgrounds in theology. Thankfully, the fruits of academic scholarship have become increasingly accessible through both print and now electronic resources.

- The process of study deserves careful consideration. Possible study resources should be evaluated and a priority of acquisition established. Financial and time budgets must be carefully planned.

- A leading educator of a bygone generation stated the law of the teacher as follows: "A teacher must be one who knows the lesson or truth or art to be taught."[7] Some might object that a teacher is a fellow learner. The law of the teacher encourages that concept, for the teacher's learning is never complete and the process of learning involves continual discovery. However, the teacher who is essentially ignorant is of little help to anyone. As Jesus said, " 'Can a blind man lead a blind man? Will they not both fall into a pit?' " (Luke 6:39).

- The serious student will read widely. A lifelong pattern of study is first of all built upon devotional reading. It must then include study resources beyond the normal course of devotional reading. Reading should not be limited to the current requirements of teaching or other ministry.

---

[7]John Milton Gregory, *The Seven Laws of Teaching* (1884; reprint, rev. William C. Bagley and Warren K. Layton, Grand Rapids: Baker Book House, 1993), 18.

10. FAMILY STUDY AND WORSHIP AS SPIRITUAL FORMATION

Christian parents in any country should feel responsible for the spiritual nurture of their children. The parents of ancient Israel were specifically commanded to teach the Word of God's law to their children at all times.

> These commandments that I give you today are to be upon your hearts. Impress them on your children. Talk about them when you sit at home and when you walk along the road, when you lie down and when you get up (Deut. 6:6–7).
>
> Fix these words of mine in your hearts and minds; tie them as symbols on your hands and bind them on your foreheads. Teach them to your children, talking about them when you sit at home and when you walk along the road, when you lie down and when you get up (Deut. 11:18–19).

Certainly the believers in New Testament times would have fulfilled the intention of these verses far better than did their Old Testament forebears. For one thing, they lived during the fulfillment of the Old Testament prophecies, so they had a far greater sense of God's eternal plan unfolding. Also, the revelation of the Holy Spirit's power was far more widespread in the New Testament era than in the Old Testament era. With Peter's sermon in Acts 2, believers became aware that they were living during the fulfillment of Joel's prophecy of the Spirit being poured out on all flesh. Parents and children alike believed in Christ unto salvation, received the Holy Spirit, participated in Pentecostal worship, and witnessed continual divine intervention in the affairs of life. They had access both to the Hebrew canon (i.e., Old Testament) and to what was becoming the Christian canon (i.e., the Old Testament plus an increasing core of Christian literature that was already being acknowledged as Scripture [2 Pet. 3:16]). They had the teaching of the apostles, prophets, and teachers upon which to model their teaching at home. In short, they knew and understood that the power so evident in their midst was the token of God's expanding Kingdom. They could not help but convey this understanding to their children.

Today's missionary parents are privileged to continue within this apostolic tradition. The canon of Scripture is complete, and generations of its study have afforded today's panoply of study materials for every age group. The missionary also realizes the inexhaustible resource available to his family through the manifold gifts of the Holy Spirit. Martin Luther wrote, "The Spirit and the gifts are ours."[8] Pentecostal missionaries believe and teach this concept to their family. They also teach their family that "one little word" uttered in the power of the Holy Spirit is sufficient to defeat the enemy.[9] In short, the missionary family becomes a training center for an ongoing family presence in the community powerfully witnessing to the grace of Jesus Christ.

Some Western nations tend to delegate the spiritual nurture of children to the church. However, missionaries have often found that a receiving church does not have the forms of training associated with the church in the sending country. Rather than lamenting this difference, the spiritually-attuned missionary family will strengthen its times of worship until the family comes to the full measure of the stature of Christ (Eph. 4:13–14).

The benefit of being parents with a spirit of mission is that the children are encouraged to seek the graces and giftings so necessary to fulfill it. This contrasts sharply with the mindset in some countries where the church's goal for its youth seems to be spiritual conservation and clean entertainment within the program of the local church. The missionary should rejoice daily in

---

[8]Martin Luther, "A Mighty Fortress Is Our God," in *Sing His Praise* (Springfield, Mo.: Gospel Publishing House, 1991), 41.
[9]Ibid.

the privilege of raising a family in the heat of battle. Out of such surroundings, mighty sons and daughters arise to accomplish victories in Christ's kingdom only dreamed of by their parents.

11. SEEING DEVOTIONS AS RECEIVING DIRECTION FOR EACH DAY

The Christian approach to devotions is like checking with the Lord both to review general principles and to receive specific instructions for each day.

Joshua 5:13–15 gives the account of Joshua's encounter with the commander of the Lord's army. Approaching a man standing with a drawn sword in his hand, Joshua asked, "'Are you for us or for our enemies?'" "'Neither,'" he replied, "'but as commander of the army of the Lord I have now come.'" Joshua fell facedown on the ground and asked, "What message does my Lord have for his servant?" (vv. 13–14).

Note five similarities between this account and present Christian experience:

1. Joshua was part of a pilgrim people dedicated to fulfill *missio Dei*. So is the Christian today (John 20:21).
2. Joshua had already been called personally to a task within the broader scope of the mission of God's people (Josh. 1:2). So has each Christian today (1 Cor. 12:7; Eph. 4:7; 1 Pet. 4:10).
3. Joshua had already been promised the manifest presence of God as assurance of victory (Josh. 1:5,9). So has the New Testament Christian (Matt. 28:20).
4. Joshua was carefully instructed to meditate on the "'Book of the Law'" day and night in order that it might direct him in fulfilling God's mission (Josh. 1:8). This corresponds to Christian practice (Acts 2:42; 1 Tim. 4:13; 2 Tim. 3:16; 2 Pet. 1:20–21).
5. Joshua's success may be understood only in the context of the instructions he received from the commander of the army of the Lord (Josh. 5:13 to 6:5).

Even so, the success of the Church can be explained only by the counsel of the Paraclete promised by Christ (John 14:16; Acts 13:2).

It is especially in times of Bible study, praise, and prayer that the Christian may expect instructions for carrying out a personal calling within the wider framework of *missio Dei*. Joshua won his victories by following orders, even orders as strange as repeatedly marching around Jericho. Likewise, the Great Commission will be fulfilled to the satisfaction of the Christ who gave it as the Church obeys His Spirit's strategy. That strategy is best determined within the context of a daily diet of God's Word and prayer. Needed guidance often will come from the direct commands or principles of Scripture. Specific guidance must be in keeping with known scriptural principles. Those without a scriptural atmosphere may find themselves subject to frequent confusion and error.

Much has been written on the devotional habits of Jesus (e.g., Andrew Murray, *With Christ in the School of Prayer*). Mark records, "Very early in the morning, while it was still dark, Jesus got up, left the house and went off to a solitary place, where he prayed" (1:35). What some overlook is the result of that prayer. Though the apostles were looking for Jesus because of the popular demand to see Him, His response was that it was time to move on and preach elsewhere (1:38). How did Jesus know it was time to move on? The text includes a revealing line: " 'That is why I have come' " (v. 38). Something in His prayer session clarified His immediate course of action on the basis of His stated mission (purpose statement).

Missionaries with habitual prayer times tend to make the right decisions in life for the same reason Jesus did: They frequently and prayerfully revisit their purpose. Within this context, they hear the voice of God. No wonder Jesus could say, "'The one who sent me is with me; he has not left me alone, for I always do what pleases him' " (John 8:29), or " 'I have brought you glory on earth by completing the work you gave me to do' " (John 17:4). This same sense of knowing the plan of God and being completely submitted to the role He has assigned within that plan also explains Jesus' refusal to call for deliverance when He faced the agony of the cross. " 'Do you think I cannot call on my Father, and he will at once put at my disposal more than twelve legions of angels? But how then would the Scriptures be fulfilled that say it must happen in this way?' " (Matt. 26:53–54). It also explains the secret shared by the heroes of faith in Hebrews:

> "Women received back their dead, raised to life again. Others were tortured and refused to be released, so that they might gain a better resurrection. Some faced jeers and flogging, while still others were chained and put in prison. They were stoned; they were sawed in two; they were put to death by the sword. They went about in sheepskins and goatskins, destitute, persecuted and mistreated—the world was not worthy of them. They wandered in deserts and mountains, and in caves and holes in the ground. These were all commended for their faith, yet none of them received what had been promised. God had planned something better for us so that only together with us would they be made perfect" (Heb. 11:35–40).

In our times, this passage explains why missionaries leave family and country, enter environments inhospitable to the gospel message, and are willing to remain there even until death. They are among the company of all ages who are distinguished by this common factor: They know their Father's will.

12. The Apostles Valued Consistent Prayer and Study

Acts tells us that the early apostles visited the temple "at the time of prayer" (Acts 3:1). This indicates that they were observing traditional Jewish hours of prayer. The Apostle Paul, despite the demanding schedule of teaching, discipling, and tent making, professed, "I speak in tongues more than all of you. But in the church I would rather speak five intelligible words to instruct others than ten thousand words in a tongue" (1 Cor. 14:18–19). The implication seems plain enough. Paul's private devotional times included extended periods using his "prayer language." That they also included study of the Scriptures is consistent with everything we know about Paul. Consider, for example, 2 Timothy 4:13, in which Paul asks, "When you come, bring the cloak that I left with Carpus at Troas, and my scrolls, especially the parchments." Commenting on this verse, Donald Guthrie writes, "But though there can be no more than speculation about their identity, the desire to receive them throws interesting light on Paul's literary pursuits, even while on missionary journeys."[10]

Nor was this only a Pauline emphasis. Peter demonstrated his knowledge of Scripture in both his inaugural sermon on the day of Pentecost and throughout his later writings. James appealed to a Scripture passage (Amos 9:11–12) to solve the Gentile controversy (Acts 15:15–21). The author of the Epistle to the Hebrews builds his entire case of a better divine economy upon the writings of Old Testament Scripture. Of course, John's writings are so Scripture-laden that their common description is "theological."

Concluding Thoughts

Suffice it to say that to be Pentecostal implies a regular devotional habit that includes serious Bible study, systematic prayers and intercession, and freedom of worship in the Spirit. Any attempt to engage in missions without having first acquired such habits will

---

[10]Donald Guthrie, *The Pastoral Epistles*, rev. ed., vol. 14 of *Tyndale New Testament Commentaries*, ed. Leon Morris (Grand Rapids: Wm. B. Eerdmans, 1990), 185.

predispose the missionary to spiritual defeat, carnal bickering, and nonproductive or misdirected ministry.

STUDY QUESTIONS

1. Explain why succeeding in developing a healthy devotional life is called "the key to everything a missionary hopes to accomplish."
2. Comment upon the six benefits of an adequate devotional life that are given. Which of the benefits have you seen developing in your experience? Which benefits would you like to see?
3. Comment upon the insights that are given on how to realize devotional objectives. Which of these insights most reflect your own spiritual growth? In which areas do you feel the greatest need for further growth?
4. Explain why the text concludes that "Any attempt to engage in missions without having first acquired such (devotional) habits will predispose the missionary to spiritual defeat, carnal bickering, and nonproductive or misdirected ministry."

Chapter 13:

Missionary Call

Typically missionaries believe they are fulfilling a divine call. Their appointment depended upon convincing a board that such a call was genuine, and their continued support depends upon demonstrating the fulfillment of that call. Yet, in common with such important doctrines as the Trinity, when it comes to a clear description of such a call, the Bible seems strangely silent. What then is a missionary call? I will consider two points, moving from the general to the particular.

First, the missionary call rests upon the foundation of *missio Dei*. At this level, the missionary shares a calling with all true followers of Christ. That calling is to participate in *missio Dei*. God will bless all nations through Jesus Christ, the long promised seed and heir to the throne of David. His Kingdom will include those from every nation, tribe, language, and people, and it will last forever. The Church in all ages has been mandated to announce the good news of Christ's kingdom to the whole world. As it does so, it is to move in compassion and holiness, ministering transformation and anticipating the successful completion of its mission and the return of the King.

Second, the missionary call is an individual matter. At this level it is important that a missionary feel a call. This is the call to personal involvement, the level of deliberate investment of one's life in cross-cultural ministry. Divine compassion for alienated and rebellious humanity must flow across barriers of ethnicity, language, and culture. Historical prejudices must be overcome. Demonic deception must be directly encountered. The perils of danger on the one hand and, on the other, boredom, the tediousness of just trying to maintain life, will have to be faced. Many missionaries become exasperated over the time necessary just to locate cooking gas, food, and whatever else may be needed. Add to this the waiting in offices and completing reports—sometimes the feeling of being inefficient or ineffective sets in and discouragement results.

Through all this, the missionary falls back on the certainty of the calling. Consequently, two questions must be addressed: "How does this calling come?" and "How does this calling function?"

How the Calling Comes

As to how the calling comes, the key concept to understand is that there is no single pattern that fits all callings. The following points, however, may help anyone struggling with this matter:

- When Jeremiah heard his calling, he was told that it had been placed upon him before he was born (Jer. 1:5). We know that God plans the lives of His own, and it is consistent with Scripture for an individual to recognize that a personal calling predates birth.
- Isaiah was a young man worshiping the Lord in the temple when he received a mighty revelation of God's glory and heard a voice asking, "'Whom shall I send? And who will go for us?'" (Isa. 6:8). Isaiah responded in the words of a servant, "'Here am I. Send me!'" God then answered, "'Go and tell this people . . .'" (Isa. 6:8–9). From this, one may infer that a specific calling can come to those who approach the Lord in worship. Also, specific callings often come to those who have answered a more general calling. An illustration of this concept is in Acts 16:6–10. In this account, Paul and his team traveled throughout

Phrygia and Galatia and were forbidden to enter the provinces of Asia or Bithynia before being directed through a vision to go west to Macedonia. In the Old Testament, it was Abraham's servant who acknowledged, " 'As for me, the Lord has led me on the journey . . . ' " (Gen. 24:27). Though from diverse settings, these texts demonstrate that the needed guidance (call) came while engaged in obedient service.

- Jesus called the disciples as they went about the task of making their living. Most of them were fishermen. From this example, one may conclude that Jesus still calls people as they go about the business of living.
- Saul of Tarsus was called as he traveled to Damascus to arrest believers. We may conclude that the Lord even calls His workers from among His enemies.

How Callings Function

The primary point to remember about how callings function is that they are all related to the realization of Christ's kingdom.

It is important to recognize that calling to any kind of service within the kingdom of Christ comes from the King himself. Even in those cases when someone prays to be called, it is the Spirit of God that prompts the desire for that prayer. Knowing that God is the initiator of a calling is important because such a conviction gives the missionary (or any believer) endurance during times of difficulty or delay. Since all true callings come from the King, they naturally fit into the purposes of the Kingdom. God has revealed his mission throughout Scripture, and the callings individual believers feel are means for accomplishing that mission rather than for individual recognition or a sense of fulfillment.

God provides the necessary enablements (gifts) to accomplish each individual's portion of *missio Dei* (Eph. 4:7). Ephesians 4 gives a listing of gifts given to "prepare God's people for works of service" (Eph. 4:12). Missionaries are God's gift to the Church so that it can cross all kinds of barriers and know what to do when the barriers are crossed. They may be required to function as apostles, prophets, evangelists, pastors, and teachers. Paul exhorted the young missionary Timothy, "Do not neglect your gift, which was given you through a prophetic message when the body of elders laid their hands on you" (1 Tim. 4:14). We are also to "eagerly desire the greater gifts" (1 Cor. 12:31). God's provision is more than adequate to accomplish his assignment.

Work Ethic and Perseverance

WORK ETHIC

Sometimes there is a concern in Christian ministry that work will become like leaven, working its way into all spheres of life to the detriment of personal and family well-being. No doubt there are personality types that demonstrate obsessive behavior about their work. I contend, however, that such tendencies should be considered as human behavioral problems, not as work problems. That is to say, work itself should not be blamed as though it is inherently evil. Rather, missionary service should be approached as an assignment given in trust from God, an area of stewardship to one's Lord. Paul summarizes the biblical work ethic as follows: "Now it is required that those who have been given a trust must prove faithful" (1 Cor. 4:2).

We have already acknowledged the problem of an environment requiring tedious hours just to maintain life. But once that is mastered, actual missionary service must be rendered; unfortunately, a missionary may direct too little effort toward actual missionary service. Missionaries want to succeed in their assigned mission; the following suggestions are offered to help that happen.

1. Determine to maintain a strong work ethic. Without going into the historical development of the term "work ethic," here are some foundations of understanding about work for the missionary.

"Work" may be defined as the systematic dedication of time and talent to accomplish a stated objective. For the missionary, that stated objective relates to *missio Dei* as given in Genesis 12:3b: "'And all peoples on earth will be blessed through you.'" In the fullness of time, Jesus Christ came to be the seed to bring that blessing to all peoples (Gen. 3:15; 22:18). It follows, then, that the predominant view of work should be that it is good, because it relates directly or indirectly to accomplishing God's purpose.

The Church has attempted in both laudable and deplorable ways to accomplish this mission through the centuries. Though historically there have been imperfections in people and methods, the Church is now resurgent with Pentecostal power, making enormous strides among those formerly regarded as unreached and almost unreachable. At the time of this writing, for example, it is reported that more Muslims have come to faith in Christ in the last ten years than in all previous history. Many feel that the Church of this generation is far closer than the Church of any previous generation to completing the twin tasks of making disciples among all nations (Matt. 28:18–20) and proclaiming the gospel to every person (Mark 16:15). This witness is being accomplished with increasing sensitivity to the Church's responsibility to minister holistically to the world's poor and suffering.

The sovereign God is calling men and women to move out into the harvest fields of the world, going literally *from* all nations *to* all nations. Jesus is building His church in the hardest places and thus accomplishing the Holy Spirit's eternal purpose of bearing witness to the gospel of the grace of Jesus Christ.

What these men and women do in these hardest places is called "work," and since it is the direct mandate of the sovereign God given through his resurrected Son, Jesus Christ, it must therefore be regarded as "holy."

The work ethic that is needed in this eleventh hour of earth's harvest goes far beyond that produced through societal factors anywhere in history. The ethic of harvest translates Christ's passion into words and deeds in keeping with the urgency of the hour.

It takes time and earnest attention to study, prepare lessons, grade papers, balance a set of books, write letters and reports, and disciple students by traveling out to preach with them on weekends. Yet national church leaders continue to plead for missionaries who are fully committed to training national leadership and who, at the same time, have the kind of ministry that results in radically changed lives.

2. Plan to succeed. One area of planning is establishing a daily schedule. A married couple must plan how to approach the tasks of work and the tasks of maintaining family and home. Since all good planning requires accountability, it only makes sense to schedule for a weekly review. Spot weak areas, think of new approaches, and find ways to succeed in the stated objectives.

3. Learn to bounce back. Even the best of plans is subject to the unexpected. The key to long-term accomplishment is often the ability to bounce back after seeming defeat. If the morning did not go well, expect a glorious afternoon. Learn from defeats and apply greater wisdom in the next approach. As someone said, "Work smarter, not harder."

4. Approach missions as ministry. Missions should always be a participation in a grand adventure, the building of a Kingdom. It is the fulfillment of a divine calling, not an occupation of one's own choosing. Let all service be done as unto Christ, and the fellowship of his suffering will be a joy, and the power of the resurrection will be a daily companion.

5. Plan for relaxation. Though each ministry has its times when there is literally not a spare minute, that should not be the norm for all seasons. It is good to

plan for family time and outings. Blessed are the missionaries who enjoy the gardens, farms, songs of the birds, and the sunsets. They will live to enjoy the sunrise.

6. Develop a keen sense of discernment and welcome the intrusions that are of divine origin. Did you ever ponder what an anemic chapter John 3 would be had Jesus been too busy to welcome Nicodemus's nighttime intrusion? Always take time to hear a story.

Those who felt they had mastered the disciplines of ministry in their home country may find themselves at loose ends in another country. There is just so much work to do. The problem is often made worse by the necessity of working from one's home. The missionary must determine to rise above the challenges and find a way to get the job done—and of course maintain a happy family. It can be done, and the price is usually a mix of determination, flexibility, and common sense. One thing is for sure: It is not good sense to train for years, go through the rigors of appointment and deputation, travel to another continent, and then perform meaningful work on only a part-time basis. Something concerning the ethics of working during harvest is missing in such cases. It should also be recognized that missions is a team effort, and those who go for years without getting their plow in the ground will come to be resented.

PERSEVERANCE

There are times when it would be all too easy to fail to see a task through to completion.

"Be patient, then, brothers, until the Lord's coming. See how the farmer waits for the land to yield its valuable crop and how patient he is for the autumn and spring rains. You too, be patient and stand firm, because the Lord's coming is near" (James 5:7–8).

As was noted in the biblical theology section, the harvest metaphors of the Bible are far more than accidental motifs owing to the agricultural background of the times. In every way, harvest is an apt metaphor for what the Lord is accomplishing through His Church on the earth. The farmer waits because he knows what will happen with the interaction between seed, soil, and rain. Even so, those who would represent the kingdom of Christ as it extends beyond present frontiers must have a farmer's patience and confidence. All the ingredients for harvest are present, and to withdraw before harvest would be contrary to logical expectation.

When perseverance is lacking, discord often results. As Max Lucado observes, "When those who are called to fish don't fish, they fight. . . . When those who are called to fish, fish—they flourish!"[1] The last-day harvest requires perseverance.

STUDY QUESTIONS

1. Why is the sense of calling a critical concern to the missionary?
2. Explain how specific callings come, mentioning the four points given in the text. Add your own insights on how callings are recognized.
3. Comment on the points that are given on how callings function. How do these points address the problem of one feeling a strong calling but lacking confidence to fulfill that calling?
4. How may work be defined? What attitudes toward work should mark the missionary candidate?
5. In your own words, summarize and apply the warnings that are given concerning missionaries who are unable to realize a meaningful level of work.
6. Why is perseverance needed, and what difficulties result when it is lacking?

---

[1]Max Lucado, *In the Eye of the Storm* (Dallas: Word, 1991), 57.

Chapter 14:

Personal and Social Formation

Promoting a servant approach to the Philippian believers, Paul appealed to the incarnation of Jesus Christ (Phil. 2:5–11). Few would deny that incarnational ministry remains the ideal for missionary service. Hudson Taylor recognized that the Chinese of his day considered the gospel foreign. Part of the problem, he concluded, was the foreignness of dress and custom of those who came as emissaries of the gospel. From that time until the present, evangelical missionaries have grappled with the questions of cultural identity. Although a detailed treatment of this topic is beyond the limits of this study, some significant points for consideration will be mentioned.

Accepting One's "Birth Cultural Identity"

Occasionally there are missionaries who seem to lose track of their origin. But this is not necessarily a good thing. There may be instances in which a missionary's total identification is a gift from God. Nevertheless, it would be hard to argue that Jesus modeled this. He never forgot where he came from, He checked often with His Father at home (i.e., "in heaven"), and He knew where He was going when He completed His assignment. So, too, with Paul. He never forgot he was a Jew from Tarsus, a Pharisee, and a Roman citizen called by Jesus to spread the gospel to the Gentiles. In reality, few can achieve total cultural identity with another people group and such identification should not be held as an ideal.

It is far healthier to accept the cultural identity of one's birth and childhood as a permanent part of one's self-image. To reject one's heritage in favor of an alien identity probably seems strange to all peoples.

Achieving Interactive Levels Within Other Cultures

Biculturalism is a more realistic and healthy goal than the substitution of an adoptive culture in place of one's birth culture. I have always felt that the missionary is blessed who is able to move from one culture to another effortlessly, without even realizing when it happens. All who work cross-culturally should strive for cultural identification and for a lifestyle that does not give offense. The greatest indicator of this is probably the level of friendship one feels toward those of another background. This friendship, like the fellowship (Gk. *koinônia*) recommended by Paul in Philippians 2:1–4, comes about best by working together, sharing a common passion to fulfill *missio Dei.* Those who have traveled together on errands for the King achieve a degree of fellowship unknown in other circumstances. Stories that are told, explanations of life, and the lore of the campfire all unveil worldview. In my judgment, ministry shared as equals in the Kingdom is the key to achieving a healthy level of interaction with another culture.

For those who long for this mutual exchange but find it elusive, I offer the following suggestions (which I wish I had understood sooner and better).

1. Be a good listener. All the world loves to tell a story but so few have ears to hear. A Swahili saying goes, *"Haraka, haraka, hana baraka,"* which translated means "Haste, haste, with no blessing."[1] One day

---

[1]Phillip Keller, *Strength of Soul* (London: Hodder & Stoughton, 1993), 19.

when I was new to Africa, I visited a church three miles from the road. As we returned to the car after the service, the pastor asked me if I saw a certain tree not too far distant. I remember being conscious that the pastor's question was a deliberate measurement of my ability to listen to a story. Something about the way I said "yes" seemed to have passed his test. The porters with their loads of fruit thanking me for my visit walked on down the trail unnoticed. "Do you see that branch, the big one?" the pastor continued. I had passed the test, and the story began. It seems that two villages had been fighting for a long time. Tiring of the bloodshed, the elders had called that tree to witness a solemn agreement of peace. Some time later the son of the chief defied the treaty by passing "that tree" to kill a man and then "run for bush." (It was as though the story could be told correctly only by once again visually recognizing the tree.) The old chief knew war would resume and many would die. When the sun came up the next morning, the village found the chief's body hanging from that branch. There has never again been war between those two villages. It was a moving story, but if it had a symbolic meaning I missed it. Of course I thought of trying to connect the story to Jesus dying on the cross, but that did not seem to be implied. I think the point of the story was that I had time to listen to it. I had made a friend.

2. Spend time with new acquaintances in their own surroundings, where they are at home. Most teachers naturally perform best within the setting of the classroom. That's why we urge Bible school teachers to visit their students outside the classroom (e.g., in the churches they pastor). Such a policy is not designed to hinder the teacher's instruction but to enhance the teacher's listening. When a student hosts the teacher, a role reversal occurs, at least in part. Even if the teacher is invited to preach, the event is student-

centered: The student extends the invitation, handles the introduction, and hosts the hospitality following the service. The teacher has the rare opportunity to see life through the student's eyes when the student is performing well. Someone once said, "Everyone is ignorant, only just in different subjects." Incidentally, the student who fills this role of "teacher" on the weekend will be among the most attentive back in class at the Bible school.

3. Learn to recognize how nonverbal meaning is conveyed.[2] Notice how space is used: For example, how close are people to each other when they speak? How is furniture arranged? What value is placed upon the varying degrees of grouping or solitariness? Notice who speaks to whom in the exchange of greetings. Notice acceptable, questionable, and inappropriate modes of dress, considering carefully such matters as age, social standing, and occasion. Learn the times and significance of cyclic events, such as the beginning of the rainy or dry season, harvest, new moon.

4. Be alert to the fact that most societies are event-oriented. Attention has already been drawn to a common motto on Nigerian lorries (trucks): "No event, no history." Significant events are the building stones of history. Many times Westerners fail to appreciate the significance their adoptive cultures attach to events.

5. Recognize how important relationships are. Make at least one friend who will tell you the truth about the significance of environmental clues so that you understand what is meant and are understood yourself.

---

[2]The classic treatment of this subject is Edward T. Hall's *The Silent Language* (Garden City, N.Y.: Doubleday, 1959). For a helpful summary, see David J. Hesselgrave, *Communicating Christ Cross-Culturally*, 2d. ed. (Grand Rapids: Zondervan Publishing House, 1991), 424–43.

6. Never waste a crisis. When things go wrong, as they will, make amends as soon as and as well as you can; then move ahead, having learned from the experience.
7. Pray to know the difference between unwanted interruption and significant interruption, the moments to be savored.
8. Treat each person as made in the image of God. Make no exceptions.

Language Learning as a Cultural Experience

The importance of language learning is universally acclaimed. However, there are different schools of thought on the relative merits of language schools and what is sometimes called the LAMP method ("Language Acquisition Made Practical").[3] At the same time, all agree that there is a strong relational component to most language learning. For example, language learning for the purpose of conversation is to a large extent a social experience. And in fact, most of the people in the world who learn a second or third language do so in an informal context by living among those who speak it.

Another factor that must be reckoned with is the extent to which language defines experience. The Sapir-Whorf hypothesis, which holds that language imposes an inherent worldview upon culture, has been widely debated.[4] It is safe to say, however, that language learning is a key to understanding the native speaker's worldview. The very structures of language may hold keys concerning societal values and norms. Language

[3]E. Thomas Brewster and Elizabeth S. Brewster, "Bonding and the Missionary Task," in *Perspectives on the World Christian Movement*, ed. Ralph D. Winter and Steven C. Hawthorne, rev. ed. (Pasadena: William Carey Library, 1992), C-113.
[4]Hesselgrave, *Communicating Christ*, 367–73.

is learned in order to communicate ideas, but this is not the whole story. It is also learned to gain understanding of those cultural nuances that are distinctively expressed within each language.

Psychological Wholeness

The mental health field is highly specialized, and excellent resources written from a Christian worldview are available.[5] There are also several Christian counseling practices that have extensive experience in working with missionaries. I address the topics that follow not as a professional, but as a missionary; they are a statement of guidelines intended to undergird the missionary experience.

It would be nice if the call of God erased all negative influences of one's past, but this is not the case for most missionaries. So even far from home, events of the past can resurface and cause personal problems, hindering the accomplishment of the missionary's assignment. The following advice, though basic, is very important.

First, it is important that the missionary knows the freedom that comes from forgiveness. First John 1:9 states, "If we confess our sins, he is faithful and just and will forgive us our sins and purify us from all unrighteousness." No believer should live with unconfessed sin or with spiritual bondage or with addictions. If there has been willful sin, it should be repented of and renounced. The believing community will most often know how to minister freedom to those in need. Referral to a professional may be necessary if the difficulty remains. In no case should a person undertake missionary service in the hopes that deliverance may be found on the foreign field.

[5]For example, see Marjory F. Foyle, *Honorably Wounded: Stress Among Christian Workers,* rev. ed. (London: MARC, Interserve, Evangelical Missionary Alliance, 1988); Marge Jones and E. Grant Jones, *Psychology of Missionary Adjustment* (Springfield, Mo.: Logion Press, 1995).

In the case of having experienced an injustice or abuse, the believer may find it necessary to consciously forgive the offender. Jesus said, " 'Forgive, and you will be forgiven' " (Luke 6:37). Jesus also said, " 'But if you do not forgive men their sins, your Father will not forgive your sins' " (Matt. 6:15). If one is having difficulty forgiving, help should be sought from a mature spiritual counselor. For deep wounds, Christian professional assistance may be advisable. These are basic Christian issues. It is inadvisable to go into missionary work without resolving the need to forgive.

There are other issues from the past that are not matters of sinful behavior or unforgiveness. Yet, if they are unresolved, they will lessen emotional and spiritual well-being. These also should be faced personally, with trusted counselors or professionals. Any problem from the past that is troubling at home will tend to be more troubling overseas. Nevertheless, there are wonderful testimonies from those who have received help and are happy and productive in missionary service. Most mission boards will be more than supportive of one's efforts to achieve wholeness and freedom from matters of the past.

Family, Extended Family, and the Family of God

The good relationship between the missionary and immediate family members is extremely important. Three components will help to maintain good understanding among the family members serving together on the field. The first is genuine spiritual respect. All are forgiven, all are called, and all share in the mission the family have been commissioned to. Paul's analogy of the body with many parts teaches that no member of the body is to show disrespect to any other member (1 Cor. 12:12–31). No one need compete or copy in order to gain approval. The second component is communication. There simply must be a commitment of the family to communicate with each other. The family is its own support network, but the network functions only as well as its ability to communicate. The third component is spiritual fervor. The family will be greatly helped to accomplish their mission as all members maintain a commitment to the urgency and importance of that mission. Once again, Paul's analogy of the body is important. "If one part suffers, every part suffers with it; if one part is honored, every part rejoices with it" (1 Cor. 12:26). If husband, wife, or children struggle spiritually, all members of the family rally in prayer and support. When God uses any one member in some special way, the family likewise rejoice. It is not necessary for all the family members to have a public ministry, for the spiritual battle and the victory are shared by every member regardless of who may have been in the public arena.

The relationship of a missionary to family members not on the field is also important. Four areas need to be addressed. First is the matter of family members who are accustomed to serving as confidential advisors; they may wish to give long-distance advice to their relatives on the field of service. But now living far away, they literally are not in a position to offer advice about situations on the field. The missionary will do better to reserve matters of decision making for a more immediate group and maintain a cordial and informational relationship with the family member.

The second area has to do with the "leaving and cleaving" associated with marriage (see Mark 10:7). In some families, parental bonds with a married child remain very strong long after the marriage. It's possible that a parent may regard as a betrayal the married child's going to the foreign field. Such a parent, whether or not a believer, may resort to guilt tactics to keep a child from answering the call to service. Although every arrangement for parental well-being needs to be made, Scripture is abundantly clear that the calling of God is to be regarded as taking precedence over remaining home with parents. In Matthew 8:21–22 Jesus shows the priority of His kingdom: "Another disciple said to him, 'Lord, first let me go and bury my father.' But Jesus told him, 'Follow me, and let the dead bury their own dead.'" Commenting on this verse, R. T. France states, *"The dead* can only mean those outside the disciple group, who lack spiritual life, and who in the absence of a higher calling can be left to deal with mundane matters."[6] (See also Matt. 10:37–38; 19:29). Jesus himself provided an example: He made provision for His mother but did not allow His concern for her to keep Him from taking up the cross (see John 19:26; see also Matt. 10:38).

The third area has to do with extended family members during times of protracted home service (deputational ministry). Reunions should be joyful, and special family times should be planned for. Missionaries should be forewarned, however, that any family member opposed to missionary service will see in each return to the home country an ideal time to pressure the missionary to leave missions. Any ambivalence by the missionary only increases these demands; they must be resisted lovingly but firmly.

The fourth area is that of travel to the home country for weddings, funerals, and other significant events. Today, such travel is not only possible but at times quite economical. Within mission policy, each family must establish their own travel guidelines, considering their stewardship of the calling and the effect upon supporters if "their" missionaries are seen too often in the homeland.

One of the greatest joys of missionary service is the warmth of support that comes from being part of the family of God within the field of service. Once there is a national church, each missionary family should make

---

[6]R. T. France, *Matthew,* vol. 1 of *Tyndale New Testament Commentaries* (Leicester, England: InterVarsity Press, 1992), 160.

it an integral part of their lives. Each rejoices with the other in times of joy and weeps with the other in times of sorrow. They share prayer requests and testimonies, bringing the highest level of fellowship. Missionary parents hold up church leaders as ideals before their children, making sure their children hear these faithful servants preach as well as learn something of the significance of their roles within the kingdom of God. The broader mission family likewise assume roles often as close as that of natural family. Mission meetings, holidays, school experiences, and church councils all give ample opportunity for natural friendships to grow into marvelous networks of support and encouragement.

Implications of Living as a Resident Alien

Several scriptural themes deal directly with the condition of being a stranger, a foreigner, an alien. Moses seems to have considered being an alien in Midian significant, for he named his first son *Gershom*, which sounds like the Hebrew for "an alien there" (see Exod. 2:22). Exodus 22:21 exhorts, "Do not mistreat an alien or oppress him, for you were aliens in Egypt." Hebrews 13:14 says, "For here we do not have an enduring city, but we are looking for the city that is to come." Finally, 1 Peter is addressed to "God's elect, strangers in the world, scattered throughout Pontus, Galatia, Cappadocia, Asia and Bithynia." So before giving suggestions on how to live as a resident alien, we would do well to note that the general condition of aliens has not escaped the notice of the Lord. In fact, there seems to be a special place in the divine economy for this category of believer.

How can an alien not only survive but thrive? While entire books are written on the subject,[7] I will mention only a few major points here.

---

[7]Ted Ward, *Living Overseas: A Book of Preparations* (New York: Free Press, 1984).

The alien should make every effort in the new location to feel at home. Years ago, I heard an American pastor in another country announcing all services in "our time and your time." That may have indicated an absence of adjustment! Pictures should be put on the walls, the flowers planted, and yard kept. In short, the new location should look inviting, and as much as possible and appropriate, like home. That is not to say the surroundings should be made to look particularly foreign. They should, however, look like someone has come to stay.

Each person has a way of looking at life, a "normal setting," that can be adjusted, or reset. This "internal setting" should be carefully evaluated and all systems reset in such a way as to indicate "We're comfortable here and have no plans to leave anytime soon." For our first three years outside our native land, we lived where the nearest known telephone was about 120 miles away, a distance taking four or five hours to drive. The immediate result was that for three years we didn't "phone home." The long-term result? Our internal clock was reset and our new location began to feel like home to us. While I would not recommend imposing a form of isolation, one should take steps to become acquainted with the strange new environment, so that it becomes well-known and normal in the shortest possible time.

My standard advice to those moving to Africa is "Make friends with the African way." That idea can be applied to any new land. Subpoints might include the following: Learn to see some humor in situations where you feel embarrassed. Learn new ways of viewing life. Strive to understand new forms of communication, and take delight in fitting in as much as possible. Avoid spending all your time with those whose ways are like your own. Spend significant time with those whose worldview is different from yours.

Work harder than you have ever worked in your life. Really stretch yourself. Your cause is a noble one and it deserves your best effort. Then, relax and enjoy the cool evening breezes (if there are any!). Listen to stories. Spend time with pastors, farmers, and shop owners. Spend time with your family and help them enjoy all that you have come to enjoy. After all, "The earth is the Lord's, and everything in it" (Ps. 24:1), so the servants of the Lord should feel free moving about our Master's territory. Enjoy.

Healthy Evaluation and Redefinition of Norms Concerning Roles, Zones, and Use of Time

Reevaluation and redefinition have been suggested in the foregoing paragraphs. The important point to grasp is that societal norms define acceptable behavior in such things as roles, influence, and the use of time. The newcomer's "default settings" may be wrong in any one of these areas. Blessed is that newcomer who does not prematurely assign negative spiritual significance to every societal norm. Give the new norms a little time. An insightful African saying goes: "A stranger's eyes are wide open, but he doesn't see much." If something seems strange, find out what the rule is and how it can be kept.

I once received a report that a certain chief had called me "wicked." Of course, I was a little hurt until I learned that my offense had been that I had given nothing to a community improvement project. Once I had joined the villagers in giving, the word came back to me that I was now very good! Learn the accepted roles of men, women, children, and strangers and do not flout them to prove some point. Learn how the state, the village, or the churches are structured and give honor to whom it is due. "Show proper respect to everyone: Love the brotherhood of believers, fear God, honor the king" (1 Pet. 2:17). Learn the function of time within the society,[8] and be willing to adjust without being judgmental.

---

[8]Hesselgrave, *Communicating Christ*, 431–37.

Handling Ethical Issues

How does a missionary handle ethical issues in the context of unfamiliar societal values (issues that often come unexpectedly)? For example, what should be done when a clearing agent is overheard to deny that a shipment contains electronics—and really it contains a computer? Should a construction site be closed to avoid giving an inspector a small tip? How should foreign tax issues be handled if the written code does not reflect common practice? What would Christ have the missionary to do when his hired worker requests money for children's school fees, for medicine, or for fertilizer—and there has been no payment on the worker's last loan? As a basis for further inquiry and practical application, a few suggestions follow.

- The example of Christ should never be forgotten. " 'He committed no sin, and no deceit was found in his mouth' " (1 Pet. 2:22). Jesus himself, though, testified to the difficulty of the environment when He said, " 'I am sending you out like sheep among wolves. Therefore be as shrewd as snakes and as innocent as doves' " (Matt. 10:16).

- As much as possible, determine ethical guidelines in a group setting. Many missionaries would have saved themselves problems had they known and heeded what the group was thinking.

- Listen carefully to the advice and example of national church leaders. Sadly, the foreigner is sometimes judged to have failed in a situation that local people saw as a clear ethical issue. And, contrariwise, the foreigner may make a public matter of some point that is not seen as an ethical issue by local people. Without abandoning conscience, it is often prudent for one to heed the advice of elders, especially national elders.

- Seek qualified legal counsel when appropriate. Fees paid for such advice are usually an excellent investment. Incidentally, Christian lawyers and business leaders are often more than willing to serve gratis as members of boards. Their presence often gives a depth of understanding on thorny issues.

- It is not always necessary or best to know everything that is going on. Deal with reputable firms, collect accurate receipts, and as much as possible leave unasked what need not be asked. The apostle Paul spoke of eating meat "without raising questions of conscience" (1 Cor. 10:25). Paul also spoke of the impossibility of avoiding contact with the immoral, greedy, swindlers, and idolaters of this world. To avoid such contact, Paul wrote, "you would have to leave this world" (1 Cor. 5:10). I smiled when a friend referred to a businessman as being "the best of a bad lot." The missionary must deal with some of the best and some of the worst, but they are all people made in the image of God and for whom Christ died. To avoid all questionable business contacts, indeed "you would have to leave this world."

- Be willing to leave the past behind. After prayerfully seeking counsel and preparing for life in the arena, you must believe that God will guide each day as it unfolds. If something leaves you feeling uneasy, talk with the Lord, talk with a trusted friend, and leave it behind. Learn from the past, but never let the mistakes of the past keep you from tomorrow's victory.[9]

Responding to Difficult Adjustments

There are times when things are not moving smoothly and help is needed. It was Eliphaz in the Book of Job who declared, "'Yet man is born to trouble as surely as sparks fly upward'" (Job 5:7). When the general trouble of life becomes acute, dysfunction of various kinds results. Persons may become apathetic, irritable, or

---

[9]This thought is taken from a sermon by Pastor David Watson, Central Assembly of God, Springfield, Mo., March 21, 1999.

unable to complete assigned tasks. Physical illness may also result.

It is important at such times to recognize that God is not the cause of the problems. Nor are they necessarily caused by being a missionary, or by the mission administrators, or by the country of service. God is concerned for our well-being, and God's highest compliment to His children is His plan for their service within the *missio Dei.* Mission leaders may not understand an individual situation, but I have never seen a time when they did not care.

This is not to say that each individual should then feel guilty for the problems of life. It is not necessary to assess blame. What is necessary is to recognize dysfunction when it occurs and to work for wholeness within the framework of peace—peace with God, with one's environment, and with one's self. The following steps may be in order:

1. For those who are married, start by praying together over the difficulty. Singles may pray with a confidant. Often, God will show His counsel and the problem may be resolved or become manageable. That is, prayer will result in the dysfunction being dealt with so that life and ministry may resume, a process referred to in Pentecostal circles as "praying through."
2. If outside help seems to be needed, consider first the help that is available within a local or nearby setting. These days, missions organizations recognize the need for counseling, and periodic visits of highly qualified counselors to mission settings are becoming increasingly common. Do not overlook the possibility of receiving life-changing help through the ministry of national believers. While there may be some situations that are best kept private, the fact is that severe dysfunction is self-advertising and church leaders may already be aware of the situation. If nationals with similar problems are routinely

brought to health through local ministries, do not deprive yourself of the benefits of their ministries—be it prayer ministry or professional counseling.
3. When referral to outside help is needed, it should be sought. Those serving under a mission should feel no embarrassment at making known their need for assistance. Mission boards are compassionate and will be supportive.

STUDY QUESTIONS

1. Comment on the phrase, "Biculturalism is a more realistic and healthy goal than the substitution of an adoptive culture in place of one's birth culture."
2. State the eight suggestions given for achieving "interactive biculturalism." Summarize the essential attitudes embodied in these suggestions.
3. Why is language learning called a cultural experience? What attitudes should a missionary bring to the process of language learning?
4. Comment on the suggestions given for achieving psychological wholeness.
5. Evaluate the suggestions given for learning to live as a resident alien. What is meant by resetting the "internal clock" by which one looks at societal norms?
6. What are the key points that should be remembered in handling ethical issues within a foreign context?
7. What is meant by "dysfunction" in missionary adjustment? What should a missionary do if there is reason to suspect that oneself or someone within the missionary family may be experiencing dysfunction?

Chapter 15:

The Missionary Task

Throughout this study, the focus has been upon the *missio Dei* as being the main engine that should drive all mission activity. God's mission is broad, but it is also focused. We know where God's mission is heading by looking at how it concludes. There will be "a great multitude that no one [can] count, from every nation, tribe, people and language" (Rev. 7:9). Loud voices will declare, " 'The kingdom of the world has become the kingdom of our Lord and of his Christ, and he will reign for ever and ever' " (Rev. 11:15).

The means for participating in *missio Dei* are indeed extremely varied. It is important that those within a specific ministry see themselves as members of a team, including those from all other ministries. The power of the mission comes with the true unity that is borne of mutual respect and support. On most fields, ministries overlap. A Bible school teacher, for example, may be involved in children's ministries or compassionate outreach. A health care worker may have a background as a Bible school teacher. Nearly all ministries utilize literature and media tools. A few of the many ministries now taking place are listed below.

Church Planting

Missionaries must never lose sight of Christ's declaration, " 'I will build my church' " (Matt. 16:18). It is my

239

position that this is a controlling statement when it comes to mission strategy. Building the Church is the immediate object of mission. From the Church, as it is built, the ministries of Christ are extended to the world so that Christ's quotation from Isaiah is realized: " 'The Spirit of the Lord is on me, because he has anointed me to preach good news to the poor. He has sent me to proclaim freedom for the prisoners and recovery of sight for the blind, to release the oppressed, to proclaim the year of the Lord's favor' " (Luke 4:18–19).

While God uses many means to accomplish His purposes, the Church is His primary agent, central to the accomplishment of His plan. The proclaiming and healing ministries representative of God's heart are therefore central to the mission of the Church. The starting place for missions, then, is simply the extension of the local church—throughout its immediate environment and onward throughout the entire earth. Consequently, the process of church planting is central to the mission statement of any national church anywhere in the world. To fail to have a plan for opening new churches, or cells of believers, is to signal betrayal of the mission of God.

Most churches are opened through the vision, hard work, and oversight of a local church or group of churches. It is my contention that all missionaries should see themselves as being in the vanguard of church planting regardless of what their day-to-day assignment may be. I once listened as a pastor of a large church in Africa recounted a trip to a nearby country during his early years of ministry. What amazed him was to see at least five missionaries sitting in a Sunday morning service. Though years had passed, the amazement would still come to his face when he recalled the experience. He felt that missionaries should be out planting churches.

If most new churches are planted through local church initiative, how can foreign missionaries be involved in this process? First, they must be careful not to supplant local church initiative. If a church is active, they may help by fanning the flame. The objective is to have local leadership in the church planting process, and for a missionary to preempt a healthy church-planting program will prove to be a mistake in the long run. That having been said, it should be noted that in numerous places local churches do not have a healthy approach to church planting. In such cases, the missionaries' objective is to see the birth of a church planting movement. Even though this may be done by direct missionary involvement, it is best if this involvement comes under the local or national church. Otherwise, the churches that are started will belong to the missionary, and the established church will have moved no closer toward a church-planting vision.

There may be cases in which the only way for a particular tribe or village to be entered is for the missionary to go himself as the primary church planter. Even so, care must be taken that the pioneering effort is connected to the national church through fellowship meetings, giving to the national church, and participation in other church programs. If there is no national church, it is recommended that churches be planted in small clusters so that early on the new believers take responsibility for running their own services and do not lean too heavily upon a foreign missionary.[1]

Church planting is often accomplished through church-planting crusades.[2] In most cases, these are fairly simple, low-budget events in which the gospel is preached to a crowd made up mainly of people who are

---

[1]See Melvin Hodges, *The Indigenous Church* (Springfield, Mo.: Gospel Publishing House, 1953), 47.

[2]Some object to the word "crusade" because of its possible association with the Crusades of medieval history. No doubt this word should not be used in some contexts. It is, however, used by national churches in much of the world.

not from the church. A clear message of the gospel is presented through song, testimony, and preaching. An invitation is given, and those who respond are prayed for collectively and individually. In some parts of the world, it has been customary for church planting crusades to continue for six months or longer. Extended church planting crusades have been especially successful in Latin America. While many missionaries will occasionally participate in a church planting crusade, a few make crusade ministry their life's work. These persons have been used by God to open many churches through their crusades and the crusades of those they have helped to train.

In Pentecostal practice, it is customary to pray for the sick as part of the crusade service. When demonic manifestations occur, pastors or trained lay leaders deal immediately with the people who are affected. The testimonies of those delivered from sickness and demonic attack give great credibility to the preaching of the gospel, much as they did during the New Testament era. I have heard it suggested that gifts of healing are an expression of social concern among Pentecostals. Such a concept may have some validity, though most people do not think of healing in those terms. However it is thought of, ministries of healing and deliverance from demons are typical of Pentecostal church planting throughout the world.

Ministry Training: Mobile Teaching, Higher Education, Missions, Extension

In most of the world, Pentecostal churches typically emphasize the training of their ministers. Although the three-year diploma has often been the standard, in more and more countries degree-level work is either the norm or a standard option. Graduate programs are also readily available to much of the world.

The contribution of mission organizations to these programs has changed through the years. In a bygone

day, missionaries with B.A. degrees regularly trained
pastors in schools that were mission-run. In much of
the world, these schools have long since passed to
national church control; the teacher staff is made up
mostly or entirely of national staff; and these national
staff have master's degrees or are in the process of
acquiring them, or they may hold doctorates. National
churches want missionaries to do what they are not yet
able to do. For this reason, the missionary who would
train Pentecostal pastors today should have a much
higher level of formal training than those of a generation ago. In much of the world, a master's degree will
still recommend someone for teaching, but it should be
a master's degree leading to a doctorate. At the same
time, the academic qualification, important as it is,
comes second to the spiritual qualification. Whether
they hold diplomas or doctorates, teachers must be able
to plant churches, minister in the gifts of the Holy
Spirit, and personify the vision for unreached, neglected, and suffering peoples.

Since nationals do most basic-level teaching, the
role of the missionary has come to include participation in teaching teams that minister cyclically
throughout a region. In some cases, the entire school
(i.e., faculty) travels. In other cases, the heart of the
school is local, but the school counts on visiting teachers for significant teaching blocks. Those who would
minister in these teams should have adequate local
experience to demonstrate their effectiveness as teachers. A lot of people can progress through a syllabus,
but a smaller number are change-agent teachers, those
whose students will build the church and through it
the kingdom of God. Mobile teaching teams are for
those specially called and gifted for just such ministries.

Throughout much of the world, graduate training
functions differently than it does in the Western world.
It is necessary if the church is to run effective under-

graduate training programs. It is also the forum attended by church leaders as they seek to improve their understanding and skills in order to help the church fulfill its mission. In short, there is a spiritual dynamic that far surpasses what most Westerners are accustomed to. Those who would teach in these programs must be able to sense and move with this dynamic. This work is never a nine-to-five proposition. It is only for those who are quite willing to simply pour out their lives.

Another dynamic area in training worldwide concerns Two-Thirds World missionaries. A remarkable development of our time is a strong force of missionaries from countries that formerly did not send missionaries. This movement has gone on for enough years that missionaries of Western origin are now in the minority worldwide. However, Western missionaries are being asked to perform a vital ministry: that of assisting in the training of these "eleventh-hour laborers." To contribute meaningfully to this training requires the Western missionary to have a high level of both ministry experience and specialized missiological training. Such persons will facilitate the leading edge of missions in the future.

Children's Ministries

In prophesying that the Holy Spirit would be poured out on all people, Joel included " 'sons and daughters' " (Joel 2:28). Ministry to children and youth has always been a hallmark of Pentecostal practice. The primary concept is that salvation and the baptism in the Holy Spirit are to be personally experienced by the children of each new generation. In the words of Peter, " 'Repent and be baptized, every one of you, in the name of Jesus Christ for the forgiveness of your sins. And you will receive the gift of the Holy Spirit. The promise is for you and your children and for all who are far off—for all whom the Lord our God will call' " (Acts 2:38–39).

Ministry to children has taken the form of children's church, children's evangelistic crusades, and Sunday school. In parts of Africa, for example, children's churches are attended by hundreds of children, and children's pastors may be salaried members of the church staff. Some of the children's churches make use of brightly colored costumes and hand puppets, which children's workers are taught to make. With or without these means, children's churches are a dynamic way of introducing a new generation to the power of the gospel.

Children who are homeless or refugees are also being ministered to. This ministry may take the form of feeding programs, homes for the displaced or orphans, or ministry to those victimized one way or another by AIDS.

Many churches have also started Christian schools, ranging from preschools through secondary level. Though most of these programs are totally run by individual national churches, there are several programs that missionaries have made significant contributions to, primarily through vision, organization, and funding. Some of these programs have grown to provide an integrated approach to meet the spiritual, educational, and physical needs of multiplied thousands of children.

Ministry to Major Religions

Some missions are dedicated entirely to ministry to a specific religion. Others have departments working with such religions. It is increasingly recognized that understanding of a major religion does not come easily. Rather, this understanding comes largely through years of living among practitioners of that religion. Those who have devoted themselves to such ministries have a great deal to offer: helping others to meet those of different faiths respectfully and effectively. Anyone contemplating work with Buddhists, Hindus, Muslims or other major faiths should avail themselves of people dedicated to such ministries, as well as research and media resources.

Literature and Media

The last twenty years of the twentieth century saw a major literature shift as most missions moved away from printing presses and into publishing. If anything, literature is more important than ever, but now the foreign mission is seldom the printer. This is a major paradigm shift from the days going as far back as William Carey, when the self-contained mission station typically housed a printing press. Though some national churches do own presses, in most countries today the bulk of printing is jobbed out. This change means that those with a burden for literature ministry need a different set of skills. The key need, in my view, is for those with editorial expertise, a theological and an entrepreneurial orientation, and a commitment to train local personnel in editing and publishing. There is still an overwhelming need for evangelism materials on the one hand and on the other hand for training materials at all levels. Although English is widely used in much of the world, those intending to go into missions as editors should be bilingual.

The computer age has generated an electronic media revolution. Consequently, there is an overwhelming need for those with skills in audio and video production, marketing, and of course, training abilities in these fields.

Compassion and Human Need

Tragically, one of the greatest constants in the world is disaster. Natural disasters, wars, and famines regularly bring untold suffering to vast portions of the world. Added to this is the scourge of our times, AIDS. The great cities of the world all have major problems with the plight of the homeless. At any given time, the world has millions of homeless children. Many cities report homeless children in the multiplied thousands. Adding to this is the plight of those living in shanty-towns sprawling virtually around the world.

What is the church to do? Pentecostal Christians everywhere have demonstrated their concern, often in ways that are not counted and reported. Mission organizations have prioritized ministries to the suffering, and the public has responded strongly. Presently, a growing number of foreign personnel are deployed in compassionate ministries, especially in ministries dealing with children, AIDS, and health care of some kind. Community Health Evangelism (CHE) is a program requiring minimal funding in which local personnel bring significant changes to the health conditions of local communities. Churches often result from compassionate ministries of various kinds.

Construction

Interestingly, the number of long-term and short-term missionaries working in construction-related ministries continues to grow. Many of these personnel are given assignments of a few months to a few years of supervising major building projects. Others go on short-term building teams, especially for church construction. Still others work in rural areas and provide a certain amount of foreign expertise and funding, often after the local personnel meet certain criteria to receive assistance.

Tentmakers

In addition to all of the above, those with expertise in almost any field are often wanted in short-term roles. Many also find their way to the various countries of the world working for a salary from a secular firm, the United Nations, a foreign government, or a nongovernmental organization (NGO). Tetsunao "Ted" Yamamori has written extensively advocating that those who would reach the world's unreached should consider work as "God's new envoys," especially as employees of Christian NGOs.[3]

Support Ministries

In a touching display of principle, David recognized the service of those unable to participate in a frontline battle.[4] This was in keeping with the earlier command of the Lord to Moses that the soldiers and the rest of the community were to share the rewards of battle equally.[5]

Missions has always been a team effort. Those who travel to distant lands could not do so without a significant core of dedicated support personnel and those who faithfully remember them with prayer and financial support. These active personnel residing within the home country are often the unsung heroes.

Many missions have come to rely heavily upon specialized support offices usually located in the home country. Depending upon the nature of the mission, these support personnel may be involved in publications, media production, literature distribution, fund raising, medical and humanitarian concern, prayer ministries, construction, book acquisition, or training coordination. To this list should be added the administrative leaders, secretaries, as well as finance, publications, research, and computer personnel. Then there are those involved in teaching and the preparation and

[3]Tetsunao Yamamori, *Penetrating Missions' Final Frontier: A New Strategy for Unreached Peoples* (Downers Grove, Ill.: InterVarsity Press, 1993); see also Yamamori, *God's New Envoys: A Bold Strategy for Penetrating"Closed Countries"* (Portland, Oreg.: Multnomah Press, 1987). The concept of "God's new envoys" is developed by Ted Yamamori in both books. This concept redefines tentmaking to achieve specific missiological purposes.
[4]1 Sam. 30:9–10,22–25.
[5]Num. 31:25–27.

editing of books and courses in many languages. Many of these writers and editors work within international training ministries while others work elsewhere within the organization.

Those serving tirelessly as members of mission boards and committees should also be recognized. Missions as it is known in much of the world would not exist without the specialized support ministries of men, women, youth, and children. These ministries are tirelessly promoted by visionary pastors and are led by a host of lay leaders throughout the homeland and by key administrative persons within national offices.

What makes everything possible, however, are the great multitude who pray for missionaries, give systematically and sacrificially, take care of family and business matters on behalf of missionaries and participate in the missions programs of the various departments of the church. These people provide the spiritual, moral, and financial foundation without which missions could not exist. They are partners with those who step through today's open doors (Rev. 3:8), and they will be among the number of overcomers seated with Christ on His throne (Rev. 3:21) and worshipping with those from every nation as He is crowned King of kings and Lord of lords (Rev. 5:9–10; 7:9–10; 11:15–19; 19:16).

A Final Word

This study began by tracing *missio Dei*, God's declared purpose to bless all nations through the gospel of Jesus Christ, from Genesis to Revelation. Historical models of the Church's approach to missions were then examined to demonstrate their impact within their times and beyond. Finally, I considered the missionary's spiritual formation, which will be needed to face the challenge of the future. Throughout, the empowerment of the Holy Spirit to complete the Church's mission has been emphasized as of vital importance.

My prayer has been that the reader will feel an increasing confidence in the certainty that God will successfully complete his mission and an accompanying confidence that the Church of the future will represent God's mission with sincerity, holiness, and the blessing of the Holy Spirit.

The Lord of the harvest is not reluctant to pour out His Spirit upon those He calls into His service. The sanctifying power of the Spirit is greater than the power of the world which moves to block the progress of Christ's kingdom. It is possible to live an overcoming Christian life, free from habitual sin, addictions, unhealthy thought patterns, and our own self-preoccupation.

"It is high time," wrote Phillip Keller, "[that Christians] get to know Christ in the power of his resurrection life; that they can laugh at the forces of evil arrayed against them. Then in strength of soul they can go out to remove mountains in his might!"[6] Keller goes on to add, "Anything in life that is great, noble, worthwhile and enduring demands discipline, fortitude, endurance despite every difficulty."[7]

Let all who contemplate Christ's mission be filled with the Holy Spirit, be prepared to the fullest extent possible, be confident of divine blessing, and then run to the battle. And, *run to win!*

STUDY QUESTIONS

1. Describe the roles missionaries are most likely to fill in the world today. Explain the emphasis that is given to church planting and how church planting relates to all other ministries.
2. Describe the importance of an adequate support base within the home constituency for the missionary task.

---

[6]Keller, *Strength of Soul* (London: Hodder & Stoughton, 1993), 93.
[7]Ibid., 190.

Selected Bibliography

Boer, Harry R. *Pentecost and Missions.* Grand Rapids: Wm. B. Eerdmans, 1961.

———. *A Short History of the Early Church.* Grand Rapids: Wm. B. Eerdmans, 1976.

Bosch, David J. *Transforming Mission: Paradigm Shifts in Theology of Mission.* Maryknoll, N.Y.: Orbis Books, 1991.

Carpenter, Harold R. *Mandate and Mission.* Springfield, Mo.: CBC Press, 1989.

Culver, Robert Duncan. *The Greater Commission: A Theology for World Missions.* Chicago: Moody Press, 1984.

Dempster, Murray A., Byron D. Klaus, and Douglas Petersen. *Called and Empowered: Global Mission in Pentecostal Perspective.* Peabody, Mass.: Hendrickson Publishers, 1991.

———. *The Globalization of Pentecostalism: A Religion Made to Travel.* Irvine, Calif.: Paternoster, Regnum Books, 1999.

Dyrness, William A., ed. *Emerging Voices in Global Theology.* Grand Rapids: Zondervan Publishing House, 1994.

———. *Invitation to Cross-Cultural Theology: Case Studies in Vernacular Theologies.* Grand Rapids: Zondervan Publishing House, 1992.

———. *Learning About Theology from the Third World.* Grand Rapids: Zondervan Publishing House, Academie Books, 1990.

Edman, V. Raymond. *The Light in Dark Ages.* Wheaton, Ill.: Van Kampen Press, 1949.

Hesselgrave, David J. *Communicating Christ Cross-Culturally.* 2d. ed. Grand Rapids: Zondervan Publishing House, 1991.

———. *Planting Churches Cross-Culturally.* Grand Rapids: Baker Book House, 1980.

———. *Today's Choices for Tomorrow's Mission: An Evangelical Perspective on Trends and Issues in Missions.* Grand Rapids: Zondervan Publishing House, Academie Books, 1988.

Hodges, Melvin. *The Indigenous Church.* Springfield, Mo.: Gospel Publishing House, 1976.

Hovey, Kevin G. *Before All Else Fails . . . Read the Instructions: A Manual for Cross-Cultural Christians!* Brisbane, Australia: Harvest Publications, 1986.

Johnstone, Patrick. *Operation World.* 5th ed. Grand Rapids: Zondervan Publishing House, 1993.

Jones, Marge, with E. Grant Jones. *Psychology of Missionary Adjustment.* Springfield, Mo.: Logion Press, 1995.

Kaiser, Walter C., Jr. *The Christian and the "Old" Testament.* Pasadena: William Carey Library, 1998.

———. *Toward an Old Testament Theology.* Grand Rapids: Zondervan Publishing House, Academie Books, 1978.

———. *Toward Rediscovering The Old Testament.* Grand Rapids: Zondervan Publishing House, 1991.

Kane, J. Herbert. *A Concise History of the Christian World Mission.* Grand Rapids: Baker Book House, 1982.

Keyes, Lawrence. *The Last Age of Missions.* Pasadena: William Carey Library, 1983.

Ladd, George Eldon. *The Gospel of the Kingdom.* Grand Rapids: Wm. B. Eerdmans, 1959.

Latourette, Kenneth Scott. *A History of the Expansion of Christianity.* 7 vols. New York: Harper & Brothers, 1937–1945.

Liao, David C. *The Unresponsive: Resistant or Neglected.* Chicago: Moody Press, 1972.

McGee, Gary B. *This Gospel Shall Be Preached.* 2 vols. Springfield, Mo.: Gospel Publishing House, 1986–1989.

Neill, Stephen. *A History of Christian Missions.* Rev. ed. London: Penguin Books, 1984.

Petersen, Douglas. *Not By Might Nor By Power: A Pentecostal Theology of Social Concern in Latin America.* Irvine, Calif.: Paternoster, Regnum Books, 1996.

Pomerville, Paul A. *The Third Force in Missions.* Peabody, Mass.: Hendrickson Publishers, 1985.

Richardson, Don. *Eternity In Their Hearts.* Ventura, Calif.: Regal Books, 1981.

Steyne, Philip M. *In Step with the God of the Nations.* Houston: Touch Publications, 1992; rev. ed., Columbia, S.C.: Impact International, 1997.

Stronstad, Roger. *The Charismatic Theology of St. Luke.* Peabody, Mass.: Hendrickson Publishers, 1984.

———. *Spirit, Scripture, and Theology: A Pentecostal Perspective.* Baguio City, Philippines: Asia Pacific Theological Seminary Press, 1995.

Taylor, William D., ed. *Too Valuable to Lose: Exploring the Causes of Missionary Attrition.* Pasadena: William Carey Library, 1997.

Van Engen, Charles. *God's Missionary People: Rethinking the Purpose of the Local Church.* Grand Rapids: Baker Book House, 1991.

———. *Mission on the Way: Issues in Mission Theology.* Grand Rapids: Baker Book House, 1996.

Verkuyl, Johannes. *Contemporary Missiology: An Introduction.* Translated and edited by Dale Cooper. Grand Rapids: Wm. B. Eerdmans, 1987.

Vos, Howard F. *Exploring Church History.* Nashville: Thomas Nelson, 1994.

Williams, Morris. *Partnership in Mission.* Springfield, Mo.: Assemblies of God Division of Foreign Missions, 1979.

Wilson, Everett A. *Strategy of the Spirit: J. Philip Hogan and the Growth of the Assemblies of God Worldwide 1960–1990.* London: Paternoster, Regnum Books, 1997.

Winter, Ralph D. and Steven C. Hawthorne, eds. *Perspectives on the World Christian Movement.* Rev. ed. Pasadena: William Carey Library, 1993.

Yamamori, Tetsunao. *God's New Envoys: A Bold Strategy for Penetrating "Closed Countries."* Portland, Oreg.: Multnomah Press, 1987.

———. *Penetrating Missions' Final Frontier: A New Strategy for Unreached Peoples.* Downers Grove, Ill.: InterVarsity Press, 1993.

Zuck, Roy B., ed. *A Biblical Theology of the Old Testament.* Chicago: Moody Press, 1989.

Scripture Index

OLD TESTAMENT

NEW TESTAMENT

Subject Index